Penguin Books
My Music

Steve Race was born in the city of Lincoln, in the same
year that the British Broadcasting Company was formed
and Prokofiev composed *The Love of Three Oranges*.
In the circumstances it was only to be expected that he
would grow up to become a broadcaster and musician
with a fondness for fruit.

After graduating from the Royal Academy of Music he
served with the RAF during the war, then became a
freelance composer, pianist and arranger in television
and recording studios. When commercial television
began in Britain, he joined the London weekday
contractors as joint Musical Adviser with Sir John
Barbirolli. For the past fifteen years or so he has to
some extent deserted practical music-making for the
compère's chair.

Widely known as a witty journalist no less than as a
wide-ranging musical expert, Steve Race describes
himself as 'the luckiest man alive, and possibly the
happiest', as his autobiography, *Musician at Large*,
testifies. Married, with one daughter (Nicola), he lives
between a beechwood and a barleyfield in the Chiltern
hills. His hobby is driving into London as seldom as
possible.

My Music

by Steve Race

with the contributions of
Frank Muir, Denis Norden, Ian Wallace
John Amis and David Franklin

Drawings by John Jensen

The panel game originated by
Edward J. Mason and Tony Shryane

Penguin Books

Penguin Books Ltd, Harmondsworth,
Middlesex, England
Penguin Books, 625 Madison Avenue,
New York, New York 10022, U.S.A.
Penguin Books Australia Ltd, Ringwood,
Victoria, Australia
Penguin Books Canada Ltd, 2801 John Street,
Markham, Ontario, Canada L3R 1B4
Penguin Books (N.Z.) Ltd, 182–190 Wairau Road,
Auckland 10, New Zealand

First published by Robson Books 1979
Published in Penguin Books 1980

Copyright © Steve Race, 1979

All rights reserved

Set, printed and bound in Great Britain by
Cox and Wyman Ltd, Reading
Set in Monotype Imprint

Contents

Acknowledgements

The publishers wish to thank Messrs Novello & Co. Ltd, for permission to reproduce the first two bars of Elgar's *Variations on an Original Theme* (*Enigma*).

The author is grateful, almost pathetically so, for the assistance of the musicologist and opera expert Julian Budden, who kindly took time off from his massive trilogy *The Operas of Verdi*, in order to check the typescript for The Errors of Race. Mr Budden's magnum opus, though less amusing than what follows, is generally held to be more trustworthy. Still, as Shakespeare said:

> 'This will prove a great kingdom to me,
> when I shall have *My Music* for nothing . . .'
>
> *The Tempest*, III.2.154

> 'Ah – William Makepeace Shakespeare; in many ways, I feel, an under-rated playwright.'
>
> *Frank Muir*

Overture and Beginners

My Mu-sic My Mu-sic

The place: The Commonwealth Institute Theatre,
Kensington, London.
The date: A Monday evening.
The time: 7.25 p.m.

'And now here is your chairman to introduce the teams. Ladies
and gentlemen, Steve Race.'

I smooth down what is left of my hair, especially that awkward
bit at the back. I clear my throat. A final check on the zip which
I have already checked five times – one can't be too careful, can
one? Then on I go, through the centre curtains into the glare of
the television lights. The audience applauds, and I can tell from
the volume of sound that it is a full house. For *My Music* somehow it always is a full house.

'Good evening,' I say, taking my place behind the chairman's
desk centre-stage. 'Welcome to two more recordings in the
series.'

Out of the corner of my eye I can see the TV cameramen
testing their shots, the red cue-lights winking on and off as
Douglas Hespe, our TV producer, checks the pictures that will
make up his opening sequence. His videotape recording van is
parked alongside the theatre, as is the radio van which houses
our founder and producer, Tony Shryane, and executive producer Bobby Jaye.

I explain to the audience the arrangements for the evening, and then bring on my four colleagues – Amis, Muir,
Wallace and Norden – for what is known in the trade as
'the warm-up'. The intention is to warm up the audience, but

it is no less necessary for the cast to feel 'warmed up' as well.

The very way in which my colleagues walk on to the stage when I introduce them seems somehow to be revealing; a summary of their individual personalities. I bring on John Amis first. Hearing his name, John appears, and stands still for a moment regarding me, while I take in whatever items of the colourful Amis wardrobe he has decided to favour us with that evening: his red Harris tweed suit, perhaps, the emerald and silver waistcoat, or the striped jacket that always puts me in mind of a circus awning and is known as John's 'Bertram Mills'. Then he walks to his place to await the arrival of Frank Muir.

Frank loves an audience, as no doubt all performers should (though not all of us do). He steps through the gap between the television flats, spreads his arms wide and makes an elaborate eighteenth-century 'leg' for the benefit of the audience. On the way to his seat next to John, he may sing a line or two of some such song as *Ah, sweet mystery of life*. It is the grand entrance and the audience loves it. Then he sits down and rewards himself with an initial pinch of snuff.

Ian Wallace, too, is a born stage performer: naturally, given his experience as a star of the opera and musical stage. Ian is the true 'actor laddie' of theatrical legend. There is no other expression for someone so manifestly at home on the boards. His

entrance is purposeful, affable, a trifle bustling. He, too, appears centre-stage, but because my grand piano prevents his taking a direct route as the others have done, he walks forward to the footlights, then round in front of my desk and back upstage towards his own. It is a difficult 'move', as actors would say, but he accomplishes the whole manoeuvre with charm and confidence, seeming in some curious way to be facing the audience the whole time, even when he is walking upstage with his back to them.

Denis Norden, being the last in question order, is the last to be brought on. He always materializes from somewhere behind the grand piano, sliding crabwise into his place with a shy smile to the audience and a little nod to me.

It has always been like that, even in our earliest days, when the chair farthest on my left was occupied by our much lamented colleague, the late David Franklin. At our very first recording on 31 July 1966 it was David who answered the opening question. He had to identify the twenty-one repeated major chords at the end of De Falla's *Ritual Fire Dance*, and he got it right, of course.

David took part in a memorable bit of dialogue at one of our recordings in April 1972:

> STEVE: Just a quick round. It concerns famous compositions by famous people. It's quite simple: I give you a name, the name of a master composer, and you tell me whichever of his compositions comes into your mind. Right? – Ian: Wolf-Ferrari's . . . ?
>
> IAN: *Susanna's Secret*.
>
> STEVE: Fine. Now for Denis. Denis: Monteverdi's . . . ?
>
> DENIS: *Flying Circus*.
>
> STEVE: Over to David Franklin. David: Cavalli's . . . ?
>
> DAVID: *L'Ormindo*.
>
> STEVE: Right. Finally you, Frank. Byrd's . . . ?
>
> FRANK: Custard.

(After which Denis added 'Didn't that come from a suite?')

David was highly knowledgeable about operatic music, having enjoyed a distinguished career as principal bass at Covent Garden. But as the result of a throat operation his sing-

ing voice was suddenly no more, and David had to carve out an
entirely new career as a broadcaster. In *My Music* he affected a
schoolmasterly pose, adopting a manner which Denis once
described as 'David's air of outraged omniscience'. Sitting
beside him, Frank once capped a long David Franklin discourse
on some musical matter by observing, 'How can anyone not
know at such length?'

David's strong point (like Ian's opposite him and John's
since) was his splendid fund of musical anecdotes. The story,
for example, about a young English girl soprano who went to a
famous continental vocal teacher for an audition. After listening
to her sing for a while he called upon her to stop. 'My child,' he
said, 'you have a pretty voice, but you are so innocent . . . So
innocent. Tell me, child, are you – a Wirgin?'

'Yes, maestro.'

'Then go away. To be an artiste, you must love; love and
suffer. When you have loved and suffered, you will come back to
see me and I will make you great singer.'

Next morning there was a knock at the door of his studio. In
came the girl.

'It's all right now,' she said. 'Can I come in?'

David died in 1973. At less than a week's notice Owen Brannigan stood in for him, though Branny himself was far from well at the time. He, I remember, delighted us all that night by singing *Goodbye Dolly Gray* with the unexpected final couplet: 'Hark! I hear the bugle calling . . . Goodbye Doris Day!'

When John Amis joined our team at the start of the following season he must have been acutely aware of the love and esteem in which his predecessors in that chair had been held. But he combined an encyclopedic knowledge of serious music with an anything-but-serious repertoire of stories, coupling them with a quick wit of his own and an uncanny gift for imitating voices. I tried discreetly to help him a little at first with the answers, but it was hardly necessary. In any case, my idea of a helpful clue is not always of much use to its recipient. After one 'clue' (which was so obscure as to make John's task harder rather than easier), Denis observed, 'It's like throwing a drowning man both ends of the rope.'

Chairing over 300 editions of *My Music*, and devising what must by now be something in excess of 10,000 questions (good grief!), I have found that it is the sudden asides, the digressions,

that I remember with the most relish. Once, after Denis had
failed to answer a question about opera, Frank pointed out in an
injured tone that the quotation had appeared for all to see in *The
Frank Muir Book*.

> FRANK (to Denis): I sent you a copy, but you didn't read
> it, did you?
> DENIS: I told you I would read it. But I didn't promise to
> learn it by heart.

On another occasion I went to some lengths to explain how
the producer and I had achieved some special technical musical
effect by repeating two bars of the music and looping the tape
with repeated splices. 'If you've got nothing better to do with
your time. . . ,' commented Denis. And Ian Wallace remarked
thoughtfully, 'It's one of those useless occupations, like dusting
the spokes of your umbrella.' Then he added, after a moment's
reflection, '. . . or weighing the cat.'

'Weighing the cat' has passed into general usage as far as my
family is concerned, as a summary of that feeling when one is
momentarily at a loose end and feels aimless, without purpose.
'I think I'll weigh the cat.'

If any of our verbal exchanges during the programme should
strike the reader as the least bit sour or resentful when trans-
ferred to print, I must stress that we are the best of friends and
have always been so. In fact the key to our collective success has
been the genuine delight with which we greet one another at
those Thursday evening recordings. All honour to Tony
Shryane and Stan Stancliffe for the sensitive casting which
brought us together in the first place.

As David Franklin put it in his autobiography, *Basso Cantante*:

> 'Right from the start we hit it off as if the series had been
> running for years. I found it the most enjoyable work I'd
> ever done in my life. Work? I could scarcely believe my
> luck in being paid for playing the fool, and having fun
> about music, in such entertaining company.'

When Ian Wallace's turn came to write his autobiography

(*Promise Me You'll Sing Mud*) he summarized *My Music* like this:

> 'The formula was – and is – a simple one: get two profes-
> sional humorists and team each with a musical expert
> under a chairman who asks questions about music for half
> an hour. Don't make the questions too hard, accept witty
> answers as well as correct ones, allow everyone to gag and
> reminisce to their hearts' content, and realize that the
> least important aspect of the whole thing is who wins or
> loses.'

And later:

> 'We enjoy one another's company and are usually mildly
> disappointed when it's over, yet we rarely meet anywhere
> else. Steve Race must take the lion's share of the credit.
> Not only does he hold the ring with urbanity as chairman
> and contribute his share of inspired ad libbing, he also
> tailors the questions to elicit the maximum response from
> each of us.'

It is of course with the greatest diffidence and reluctance that I quote Ian's tribute to my 'urbanity' and 'inspired ad libbing', having fought (and happily lost) a battle with my equally well-known modesty. But Ian put his finger on two vital aspects of the show: the careful tailoring of the questions – why otherwise would I have asked Frank to name a composition of Byrd's? – and the fact that none of us cares a jot who wins or loses the game each week.

This last point is not always appreciated by our viewers and listeners. Why have a score at all, they counter, if the score doesn't matter? A good question: why indeed? The answer is just that panel games traditionally have points systems and we are no exception. In the immortal words of Magnus Magnusson, 'I've started, so I'll go on.' But it has to be emphasized that the contestants do not care about the marks, indeed five minutes after the end of the show they cannot remember who won or lost, any more than I can. Only a few listeners and viewers seem to carry the tally.

As to the tailoring of the questions, I remember quite early in the series thinking that I would ask Denis about a certain romantic musical comedy. 'Denis, who wrote *Viktoria and Her Hussar*?' I would say.

Then I thought again. No; not 'who wrote?' That would give him no real opportunity. In the event, I asked:

'Denis, what can you tell me about *Viktoria and Her Hussar*?' And he instantly replied: 'What have you heard?'

He went on to say that it sounded like a heavy Teutonic musical comedy and was probably every bit as arch as its title suggested. This in turn reminded him of a remark once made by Mark Twain: 'A German joke is no laughing matter.'

In order to compile the anthology of questions and answers in the pages that follow, I had to play through the archive recordings of 250 half-hour programmes. People have been known to go mad with less provocation. But I survived.

The main impression, as I came through those 125 hours of solid listening, was of the sheer brilliance of my colleagues as they answered or parried the questions I put to them week by week. If in these pages the puns seem rather thick on the ground, the reader should remember that he is holding in his hand a distillation of more than a dozen years of impromptu conversation, and that the average *My Music* programme contains a leavening of straightforward enjoyable music, as well as wit and reminiscence.

'So ends *My Music* for another week,' I find myself saying as the audience applauds another win for Ian and Denis . . . Or was it for John and Frank? (None of us can ever remember.) But as far as their chairman and question-setter is concerned, all four of them are winners, and this book is theirs. To Denis, Frank, Ian and John – and to the shade of David Franklin – my admiration and affection.

The History of Music (E. & O.E.)

Good eve-ning friends. . . .

It was the newspaper columnist Beachcomber – not one of our number, though goodness knows we would have been proud to have him – who reported a little-known fact about Wagner's aunt. She was so musical, he said, that when she came to a five-barred gate, she stopped and sang the spots on her veil.

Anyone reading that would immediately become hooked on the History of Music, and many of the *My Music* questions over the years have contributed to that history, either by bringing to light little-known facts or by inventing new ones. Our concern has been largely with familiar music, of the kind that I once saw described as 'Flagrant Hours with the Great Masters'. But we also welcome music of the sort Frank characterized as 'a very semi-known piece indeed'.

Any reader who already knows whatever there is to be known about Taglioni, the Frog Quartet or Rameses Chuckerbutty III will wish to skip this chapter. Others – read on.

The subject is ballet. What did Marie Taglioni do in 1832?

> DENIS: Did she do the splits on cold oilcloth?
> (She did not. As an experiment, encouraged by a friend, she went up 'on points' – and revolutionized ballet technique in the process.)

———

In 1823, a world-famous prima donna agreed to take part in a performance of Handel's Messiah *on condition that she was allowed also to take over the tenor arias* Comfort ye *and* Every valley. *Who was she?*

> Angelica Catalani (1780–1849), and she seems to have got away with it. On another occasion she received a fee of two hundred guineas for a single performance of *God save the King*.

———

With what do you associate the name of Carl Dolmetsch?

> With the recorder and with old instruments in general. More specifically, Denis associates the name with Extras on school bills: 'To recorder lessons: four pounds.'

———

What had Artur Rubinstein in common with John Wayne and Tom & Jerry?

> All won Oscars, presented by the grandiloquently-named Academy of Motion Picture Arts and Sciences. Rubinstein got an Oscar for his performance in *L'Amour de la vie*, the film made of his life. Gregory Peck presented the gold statuette. When someone asked him, 'Can Rubinstein really act?' Peck replied, 'Good Lord, yes. He's a better actor than I am!'
>
> Rubinstein used occasionally to visit his old friend Albert Einstein in order that they might practise sonatas together. It is reported that someone once passed the door of Einstein's music room and heard Rubinstein remonstrate, 'Oh Albert, can't you count?'

———

Who composed the Cat Fugue?

Domenico Scarlatti. The haphazard main-subject of this harpsichord fugue was said to have been inspired by the composer's cat jumping on the keys and stalking along them in the key of G minor. Chopin was supposed to have had a similar experience with one of his pets.

I myself had a budgerigar which repeatedly sang –

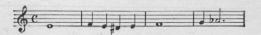

– but I was unable to make anything of it.

It should be added that whenever Frank or Denis were asked who composed the Cat Fugue, they would chant in unison 'De-pussy.' After the laughter had died down on the fifth occasion, Denis said, 'I think we ought to put a Preservation Order on that joke.'

What was the song Marching through Georgia *written to commemorate, and what did the person honoured think of it?*

Frank got this one right, though whether due to his first class Honours degree at Oxbridge or through watching late-night TV movies, I never found out. The song was in commemoration of General Sherman's march of 1864 in the American Civil War. The general hated the song, in fact he is said to have remarked that if he had known the march would inspire such a tune, he would have marched *round* Georgia instead of *through* it.

How did the Moonlight Sonata get its name?

Denis suggested that Beethoven played it over to someone and asked him, 'What does it sound like to you?' His friend replied, 'A ripe tomato.' However, as we all know, Beethoven was rather hard of hearing, and he thought his friend had said, 'Moonlight on the lake.' So he called it his Moonlight Sonata.

Denis was more nearly right than he knew. It was the poet and critic Rellstab who said it reminded him of 'moonlight on the lake of Lucerne'. The nickname was his, not Beethoven's, but the idea stuck. For myself, I have always thought the name *Rellstab* was an anagram of something or other, but have never had time to find out what.

Why is a saxophone called a saxophone?

I have always imagined this to be because it was invented by two Belgians, father and son, whose names were respectively C. J. and Adolphe Sax, the date being round about 1840. But our guest on an early *My Music* programme, the cultured and delightful Lionel Hale, made the ingenious suggestion that the saxophone might have been named after the city in which it was invented; perhaps in Glasgow, he thought. Hence the well-known line 'Roond aboot Sax we hae oor tay.'

In an antique shop I found an old violin covered in dust. Imagine my excitement when I discovered written inside it the words 'Francesco Guardi, Cremona, 1780'. How did I know that it wasn't a genuine Francesco Guardi?

Ian Wallace did not fall for my little ruse. He pointed out that Guardi was a painter, not a violin-maker.

From time to time one hears of people who really are
deceived by the signed attributions on 'old' violins.
'Made in Birmingham by Strad E. Various' does not fool
many people. But I did hear of a lady who was much
incensed to be told that a violin marked 'Guarneri,
Czechoslovakia 1738' was a palpable fake.

———

What is or was a nun's fiddle?

I confess I had not previously heard of this instrument
myself, prior to finding it in an encyclopedia. The nun's
fiddle was in fact the tromba marina, a single-string
instrument five to six feet long, so called because of its use
in convent chapels at the devotions of nuns.

Denis had a different suggestion. 'A nun's fiddle,' he
told me, 'is getting in free to *The Sound of Music* by
pretending to be one of the chorus.'

———

What do you understand by the expression Monday Pops?

Only a fool would ask Denis such a question. 'It's an Irish
slang expression for a musical instrument that you play
over the weekend and then pawn on Monday.'

Actually, the Monday Pops were popular chamber
music concerts held in St James's Hall in London on – perhaps you guessed – Mondays. (The series was immorta-
lized by W. S. Gilbert, writing his song about the punish-
ment fitting the crime: 'The music hall singer attends a
series of masses and fugues and ops/By Bach, interwoven
with Spohr and Beethoven, at classical Monday Pops.')

———

In 1737 a visiting singer from Italy so cheered up King Philip the Fifth of Spain in his melancholy that he was offered five thousand francs a year to stay on in Madrid indefinitely. He accepted, and as a result sang the same four songs to the king every night for twenty-five years. Who was this – in many ways unique – singer?

He was the famous Farinelli, unique indeed. On learning that Farinelli was a *castrato*, Ian suggested that one of his four songs might well have been *It's a great big shame*. Denis added that another might have been *I'm too shy*, at which point I hastily closed the programme before Frank could name the remaining couple of items in the Farinelli repertoire.

Which was the first opera to be recorded, and which the first symphony?

I have learnt from experience that the answer one has to this sort of question almost certainly turns out to be wrong. There is always a listener or viewer somewhere who knows better than whoever wrote the book or article from which one stole the information. But having said that, my answer to the question is that the first opera to be recorded was Verdi's *Ernani* (of all things) in 1903. The first recorded symphony was Beethoven's Fifth, in 1909, as performed by Nikisch and the Berlin Philharmonic Orchestra, while the first British symphony on records was Sir John McEwan's Solway Symphony.

The first Concerto to be recorded was an abbreviated Grieg, with Backhaus, conducted by Sir Landon Ronald in 1910. The first electrically-recorded symphony was in 1925: Tchaikovsky's Fourth.

He was twelve years old when the first gramophone records were made. Five months after his death at the age of ninety-six, his own music became available on records. Who was he?

Dr Havergal Brian. His 10th and 21st symphonies were issued on LP in May 1973. If there is anything wrong with this information I shall receive a letter from Dr Robert Simpson, musicologist and great Havergal Brian champion, to whom all inquiries should be addressed.

The star of the film Moonlight Sonata was one of the signatories of the Versailles Treaty. Who was he?

This is one of those historical events which took place at the direct request of musical quizmasters, one of whom happened to be present at the signing of the Treaty and asked whether it might not be possible for the Polish signatory to be the concert pianist Paderewski, rather than Mr Zynkzrskw Crwzicznvy, who had the pen in his hand at the time.

Rather to my surprise, Ian did not know about Mr Crwzicznvy. But he did know about Paderewski, and told us how that great artist was on his way through the artists' entrance one evening to give a concert for which he had little appetite, when a fulsome lady approached him. 'Oh Mr Paderewski,' she cooed, 'your recital is sold out and I can't get a seat.'

'Madam,' he replied, 'have mine.'

Just to clear up a simple matter, what was the first name of Rimsky-Korsakov?

DENIS: Rimsky. What else?
(Actually, Nikolai Andreyevitch.)

Who composed the Frog Quartet, and why was it so called?

Denis replied that the only Frog Quartet he knew was Les Compagnons de la Chanson. Having thus robbed our programme of its following in all French territories, he went on fearlessly: 'The Frog Quartet was composed by H. De Vere Tadpole, who managed to complete it just before he croaked.'

Not for the first time, the official reply was infinitely less interesting. Haydn composed the Frog Quartet, using a finale theme that has a croaking sound. Hence the nick-name.

———

Francis Barraud painted it about 1900. Part of the canvas was later painted out and a new section substituted. What was the painting called?

Frank was well equal to this question, having watched the picture go round at 78, 45, and 33⅓ revolutions per minute. It was *His Master's Voice*. On the original canvas a fox terrier was seen listening to Edison's Phonograph, but when Edison refused to accept the picture, the affronted artist caused the cylinder instrument to be painted out and a disc-and-horn machine substituted. The illustration eventually became the trade mark for HMV in the United Kingdom, Victor Records in America.

———

Why did Beethoven tear a strip off his 3rd Symphony?

DAVID FRANKLIN: 'Because he realized that he had mis-spelt it on the title page and had written "Erotica Symphony" instead.' For that piece of information David received half a mark. The other half mark came when he recalled that Beethoven had initially dedicated the symphony to Napoleon, but changed his mind when the latter proclaimed himself Emperor. 'So even he is no more than an ordinary human being!' Beethoven exclaimed, as he attacked the title page.

A gold disc was awarded in 1961 to a singer and his accompanist for a record they had made long before, in 1927. What was its title?

DENIS: The song was called *Forty winks*. In fact the first line went 'O forty winks, forty winks of a dove . . .' [I wonder if Dr George Thalben-Ball was listening? He was the accompanist on the famous record by Master Ernest Lough, and sometimes came to our recordings.]

The composer of O gladsome light *gave an organ recital almost every Monday for fifty years at the Church of St Michael's, Cornhill, in the city of London. Who was he?*

He was Dr Harold Darke. In the music publisher's catalogue his anthem appears with the composer's name beside it, and consequently reads *O gladsome light – Darke*. Mention of this pleasing fact led to some of the most entertaining letters I have received from *My Music* supporters, listing other anthems which, when read alongside the names of their composers, form an illuminating sentence. Among the literally scores of examples sent in, I particularly enjoyed:

> *The Lord God is a light – Green*
> *As Moses lifted up – F. Gostelow*
> *I beheld and lo – Blow*
> *Art thou weary – C. H. Lloyd*
> *Behold I bring you – J. Maude Crament*

From the deep I called – Spohr
Hide not thy face – Kellow J. Pye
I will go unto – Dr Gauntlett
Behold the name – H. Elliott Button

– not forgetting the one that also lists the price of the anthem:

And the Lord gave – Mendelssohn – fourpence

———

What is the origin of the phrase 'Let the people sing'?

Denis didn't know, but it prompted from him a genuine memory. Many years ago, he said, he had come across an outburst in a provincial newspaper, a purple piece in which the editor was highly incensed about a ban that had been placed on an outdoor performance by a local brass band. The editorial ran: 'Is this the spirit that won the war? Is this the gaiety for which the Yeomen of England are so justly famed? Is this a new kind of censorship which is to afflict post-war Britain? Strip off the bonds that bind us! Let the people snig!'

Was it perhaps Marie Antoinette who originated the phrase? On being told that the people had no bread, she said 'Let them eat cake.' When informed that they had no cake either, she remarked brightly, 'Well then, let the people sing!' Told that they had no songbooks either, she lost interest. At any rate, some centuries later, Noel Gay (whose real name was Reginald Moxon Armitage) contributed a song called *Let the people sing* to Cochran's revue *Lights Up*.

———

What was shared by Benjamin Britten, Cecil Sharp, Rameses

*Chuckerbutty III, Charles de Gaulle, André Gide, George Eliot
and the travel agent Thomas Cook?*

They were all born – unlike St Cecilia – on St Cecilia's
Day, 22 November.

---

*Chopin composed his F Minor Concerto using a piano owned by
Prince Radziwill, a piano which had what we would consider to be
rather unusual pedals. What was so odd about them?*

DENIS: Were they perhaps on the other end of the piano? –
That really would have been unusual. Or was it that his
close friend and constant companion George Sand had
knitted him, as a surprise, a pair of pedal-cosies? I suppose
that's it; he looked down and was surprised to see the only
Fair Isle pedal-cosies in Europe.

The reader may feel that there is rather a lot of Denis
Norden in this chapter. Maybe it is because he knows
more about the history of music than his colleagues. Anyway his answer to the Chopin question was entirely satisfactory (though wrong) and gained him a mark. He might
have added that Prince Radziwill's piano had knee-
operated pedals, instead of the usual foot-operated ones.

Talking of Denis:

*'Joshua fit de battle of Jericho . . .' Where do we read about the
Battle of Jericho?*

DENIS: In a book called *Great Battles of the World*. As
precisely as I can give the answer, you'll find the Battle of
Jericho somewhere between the Siege of Alium and the
Relief of Lucknow.

What are keeners?

I think it was Frank who suggested that keeners were cleaners who had got the L out of it. But he went òn to work his way towards the real answer, which is that keeners are people who keen. (An amazing deduction, when you come to think of it.) Keening is the act of singing or wailing a lamentation; a *keen* being an Irish funeral song.

As John M. Synge so truly observed, 'And him keening like the Widow McGufferty of Killamuck, the saints help us all.' (Discuss this.)

———

A last helping of Nordeniana ends this chapter. A famous violinist played at a Dublin concert in 1831. The audience insisted that he stand on the piano to play rather than beside it, so that everyone could see him. See who?

DENIS: Well, at least it wasn't as messy as if he'd stood on the violin to play the piano. Could it have been Paganini? It was.

Opera

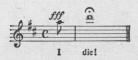

I   die!

'I do not mind what language an opera is sung in, so long as it is in a language I don't understand.'

Sir Edward Appleton

'Whenever the subject of opera crops up,' said Denis in one of our programmes, 'I feel I ought to have a note saying "Excused arias".' Certainly Denis's knowledge of opera is not so exhaustive as his knowledge of, say, cybernetics or the history of Lithuanian milking stools. Nevertheless he was able to grace our very first trial programme with a memorable operatic translation:

What is the meaning of La donna è mobile?

La donna è mobile means 'the bird's got a motor bike'.

I am not notably an opera addict, though like all music lovers I have had some wonderful evenings in the opera house. I sometimes find difficulty in following the plots of well-known operas; a fact which will be mirrored in some of the questions which follow. An eager member of the audience as I enter the theatre, I have some problems over the suspension of disbelief, more especially when the timing of musical action seems at extreme variance with the timing of action in real life.

Fleeing from an adversary, it seems to me that two people ought not to take nine minutes to cross the width of the stage. After an evening at the opera I sometimes feel like the lady I overheard once when leaving a performance of Shakespeare's *Tempest*: 'So much to admire; so little to enjoy,' she remarked. Sometimes, I said, sometimes. But what wonderful experiences were mine on the other nights! – At my first *Turandot*; at the immediately pre-war Covent Garden *Ring* cycle; at *Peter Grimes*, and (yes) at Menotti's *The Consul*. As for *Dido and Aeneas*, I was unable to include *When I am laid in earth* in my choice of records for Roy Plomley's *Desert Island Discs*, for the simple reason that I can never speak after listening to it, so be-lumped is my throat. But enough of me. On with the questions.

What have the two operas Lucia di Lammermoor *and* La Jolie Fille de Perth *in common?*

DENIS: Neither title includes the letter Z.
(And how could any chairman deny it? Memo: be more careful how you phrase the questions, Steve.)
Both operas were based on stories by Sir Walter Scott, with music respectively by Donizetti and Bizet.

———

The initial production of a Rimsky-Korsakov opera was banned. Which opera, and what was it about?

It was the story, suggested Frank, of a peasant who fell desperately in love with Catherine the Great, but un-fortunately she didn't share-ezade. With a little assistance from John Amis, Frank amended his answer to read *Le Coq d'Or*. (It was banned because it 'mocked despotism', or words to that effect.)

———

When rehearsals began for the first performance of a certain Verdi opera, the leading tenor found a blank page in his score – a complete aria was missing. Which aria, and why?

They knew this too. *La donna è mobile* (*Rigoletto*) was the aria. Verdi did not want it to leak out before the premiere, since he well knew that it was going to stop the show. Accordingly the tenor received his part the day before the dress rehearsal. On opening night, as its composer had anticipated, it was the hit of the show.

What did Napoleon open in September 1973?

'A boutique?' asked Ian hopefully. No: it was the Sydney Opera House, which opened with Prokofiev's *War and Peace*, Napoleon being one of the characters.

Frank, recently returned from an antipodean visit, had admired while there the highly distinctive appearance of the Sydney Opera House. He told us that the Sydney taxi drivers call it 'the nuns' scrum'.

When we mention the opera La Bohème *we usually mean Puccini's work. But another famous composer also wrote an opera called* La Bohème, *and some people even preferred it in its day to Puccini's work. Who was the composer?*

Leoncavallo, composer of *Pagliacci*. His *Bohème* was well received, but suffered by being produced in 1897, only a year after Puccini's version.

Who put Maxim's on the musical map?

Franz Lehár with *The Merry Widow*. According to legend, Lehár is supposed to have run up a large dinner bill at Maxim's in Paris and then found to his dismay that he was unable to foot the cost. 'Never mind,' he told the management, 'I will go home now but I will repay you a

thousand times over.' Later, true to his promise, he wrote
I'm going to Maxim's.
(DENIS: 'I tried the same trick at Fred's caff, but they
wouldn't wear it.')

When a play called The Attaché *was turned into an operetta it
became enormously successful. In fact on one particular night it was
playing in four hundred different theatres, five of them in Buenos
Aires! What was its name?*

The Merry Widow. And while we're on the subject:

*Can you name the six most delectable grisettes at Maxim's, accor-
ding to Count Danilo?*

Lolo, Dodo, Joujou, Cloclo, Margot and Frou-frou.
('That makes eleven,' said Frank. 'Who were the other
twenty-seven?')

Where would you find Ping, Pang and Pong?

In Puccini's *Turandot*, Ping being the Grand Chancellor,
Pang the general purveyor and Pong the chief cook. Frank
ingeniously suggested that you might find Ping, Pang and
Pong in the percussion section of an orchestra if the
triangle player had an instrument of unequal sides.

---

*What links Hederl, Haiderl, Hannerl, Tilly, Willi, Lili, Mitzi,
Fritzi and Kitzi?*

So far from being litter-sisters at a poodle parlour, they
are the three sisters whom Schubert loves in the various

romantic versions of his story: *Lilac Time, Blossom Time*,
and *Das Dreimäderlhaus*. No wonder he never got that
symphony finished.

———

*Where might one find Aesculapius Carboy, Eliza Smith, Thomas
Brown, Letitia and Mr Grinder?*

In Sullivan's *The Zoo*, first performed at the St James's
Theatre in 1875. The action was set between a refresh-
ment kiosk and the bear-pit at London Zoo, and even
Sullivan did not think much of the work. Ian appeared as
Mr Grinder in a radio performance, but he rather liked it,
I think.

———

*Which is the odd man out: Parsifal, Titurel, Gurnemanz and
Klingsor?*

Parsifal, a tenor, the others being basses, in Wagner's
Parsifal. I have always had a sneaking admiration for
Gurnemanz, who is described at the start of the score as
'elderly, but vigorous'. Bully for him.

———

Who composed an opera called The Pig-headed Peasants?

Quentin Hogg, thought Frank. Wrong (but neat); it was
Dvořák.
   John Amis maintains that Dvořák was of Irish extrac-
tion, his name being originally D. V. O'Rorke. O'Rorke
pre-dated that other Amis-inspired composer who emi-
grated from Ireland to Hungary, K. O'Daly.

———

Where will you find Doctor Bartolo?

I suppose there are various possible answers, but the one I wanted (and got) was 'In *The Barber of Seville*'. Ian played the role many times, and recalls how he went into the opera house one night, confidently thinking that he was about to play the good Doctor Bartolo for the ump-teenth time. 'I was sitting happily in my dressing-room,' he told us, 'when I heard a voice on the loudspeaker say "Good evening, ladies and gentlemen. Here is the cast for *Tosca* this evening. The Sacristan – Ian Wallace . . ." It so happens that the Sacristan is on about five minutes after the rise of the curtain. And there was I, in the wrong make-up, with my vest half-way over my head and Bartolo's music running through my brain. It was a nasty moment.'

I should have asked him: did Bartolo marry Angelotti in the end?

For what voice did Mozart write the part of the Pasha's steward in The Seraglio?

David Franklin told us: 'This was a really kinky piece of casting on Mozart's part, when you reflect on what usually tended to happen to people who worked in harems. (FRANK: 'You had to be cut out for the job, didn't you?')

In the end we got the thing sorted out: Osmin is a bass. Indeed, one of the most memorable of all Osmins was David Franklin himself in his operatic days.

The Habanera *from* Carmen: *what is the meaning of the word Habanera?*

On this one occasion Denis gave the correct answer and it

was left to the chairman to come up with a fanciful notion.
Denis replied correctly that the word meant 'from
Havana'.

Having looked the matter up in my Spanish dictionary
I was able to suggest that *haba* means a broad bean, while
era is a vegetable patch. So *habanera* means a broad bean
in a vegetable patch. And very tasty too, with a jug of
sangria.

Any mention of Faust *always results in Frank singing under his
breath 'Faust you put your two knees close up tight . . .' When order
is restored, the chairman can ask some run-of-the-mill question
about the opera. Like, for instance, whose poem was it that inspired
Gounod's version?*

Goethe's poem. (Of which the first line was 'Faust you
put your two knees close up tight . . .' said Frank.) Order
having been restored yet again, John Amis recalled a performance of Gounod's *Faust* in County Cork. At the end,
Mephistopheles has to go down into the depths under the
stage, and for this purpose he has a trapdoor let into the
boards. At this particular performance he pushed repeatedly at the trapdoor, but it would only move an inch
or two. He was still trying to shift it when a rich Irish voice
from the back of the theatre called out, 'Glory be to God,
hell's full!'

What does 'Nessun dorma' mean?

DAVID: It comes from *Turandot* and it means 'None shall
sleep'. When it's sung as loudly as most English tenors
sing it, you know why!

Where would you find a travelling minstrel who plays with his gusli?

Despite the subtly-concealed temptations offered by my question, David correctly identified this as a reference to *Sadko* by Rimsky-Korsakov. A *gusli* (as he also knew, though I can't think that the information did him any good) is a Russian zither. I was able to add that to me, *Sadko* always sounds like a firm of Russian undertakers.

———

Die Fledermaus: *what does it mean, and why is it called that?*

This question is an old stager where musical quizzes are concerned, though I doubt if other musical quizmasters received anything like the answer I did. It was Denis who worked his way to it. '*Fledermaus* means a bat. And a bat is called a bat because when Adam named the animals he pointed at one of them and said, "Shall we call that an omnibus?" But Eve said, "No, something else will come up that we can call that. Call it a bat." So they did.'

I suppose I must drag through the answer as to why *The Bat* is called *The Bat*. Before the action of *Die Fledermaus* begins, a Doctor Falke has gone to a Fancy Dress Ball disguised as a bat, has got drunk, fallen asleep, and has had to walk home through the morning streets dressed in his bat outfit. Now read on, or rather listen on, to Strauss's operetta.

———

Who composed the opera Lucrezia Borgia?

FRANK: Some poison or poisons unknown.
(Or if known, Donizetti.)

———

What are the opening words of Faust?

'Faust you put your two knees . . .'

Where did the story of Rigoletto *originate?*

From *Le Roi s'amuse* by Victor Hugo. John reported to us delightedly that he had come across a misprint in a record catalogue, in which the title was listed as *Le Roi s'abuse*. This was followed by various conversational exchanges which our producer subsequently cut out of the tape.

At the very end of Rigoletto, *as the heroine is dying, Rigoletto's final line is sung very loudly. Why, at such a moving moment?*

David was ready for this. 'Probably,' he observed, 'because the orchestra is playing so loudly.' (Actually, Rigoletto is calling out that by her death the curse of Count Monterone has been fulfilled.)

Ian recalled that an Italian soprano once played the part, despite the fact that she was (in his words) 'a very big girl indeed'. After being murdered, she has to be carried off stage in a sack by Sparafucile. The poor singer playing Sparafucile found himself utterly unable to shift the sack once she was in it, so for performances in which the lady took part it was arranged that Sparafucile, the hired assassin, should have three burly brothers, who came on at that point in the story to help him with his burden. In spite of this, on some nights even the four of them couldn't manage her, and then the audience could see two little legs poking out of holes in the sack, twinkling along by way of help.

David remembered having similar trouble with a well-

built soprano at Glyndebourne. 'I can't shift her,' he told
the producer in rehearsal. 'Never mind, leave it to me,'
the producer told him. And walking down into the stalls
he called out 'Taxi . . . Taxi!'

---

*Where would you find horses, rams, a bear, a toad, a serpent, a
dragon and a pair of ravens?*

My answer would have been 'In our garden shed when I
was five.' But the musical answer is in Wagner's *Ring*. At
one memorable performance the dragon's costume failed
to turn up, because it had been sent to Beirut in error,
instead of to Bayreuth.

While we are on the subject of Wagner:

What were Woglande, Wellgunde and Flosshilde doing in the water?

FRANK: They were performing Gene Kelly's *I'm singing
in the Rhine*.

---

*What would you call the story of an Irish princess and a knight in
Cornwall?*

'How about *Pelléas and Mevagissey*?' offered Denis on the
spur of the moment. When pressed for more information, he commented that 'An Irish princess and a knight
in Cornwall' sounds like first prize in a newspaper
competition. (Or if you don't want them, you can have
something else in Looe.) My answer, and presumably
Wagner's if asked: *Tristan and Isolde*.

In which opera does the leading man cry, when the leading lady tries to kiss him: 'Never, daughter of Sodom, never!'?

Ian confessed that he was no good at this sort of question, and went on to give the reason. 'My type of singer never plays the part of anyone that gets to kiss the soprano. We basses and bass-baritones never get the girl. We always have to play a drunken monk or someone's uncle. The nearest we ever get to kissing the soprano is giving her a chaste peck in Act 3 for something the tenor did to her in Act 1.'

The leading man who tells his leading lady that he doesn't want her kiss is John the Baptist in Richard Strauss's *Salome*.

Operatic plots really can be a bit far-fetched. Take Donizetti's *The Daughter of the Regiment* as an example. Marie is a foundling who has been brought up by soldiers (or perhaps by the soldiery, which sounds grosser and therefore more interesting). When a mountain lad is caught lurking round the army camp he is seized as a spy. But little Marie says 'Spare him, for it was he who saved me from falling over a nearby precipice.' In fact she wants to marry him.

Denis, what do you think happened next?

DENIS: You mean there's more? Ah yes, I remember now. His name is actually Precipice Ricardo, which is the Italian for Cliff Richard. Later in the story he marries little Marie and to avoid the precipice they take the circular route, hence the aria *She'll be coming round the mountain when she comes*.

Should any student of opera be concerned after all that to know the real answer, the mountain lad enlists and Marie is taken away to learn polite un-soldierly manners.

---

*In which opera do we learn that before the story even opens a
leading character's younger brother was bewitched as a baby by a
gipsy who was burnt alive for her crime and whose daughter intended to burn the baby in revenge but killed her own infant instead?*

> FRANK: Would that be *White Horse Inn?*
> (When it was explained to him that the grim plot concer-
> ned *Il Trovatore* Frank commented, 'Well, I'm not sur-
> prised he felt ill.')

———

Where in music would you find the beautiful lordly ones?

> In Rutland Boughton's *Faery song* from his opera *The
> Immortal Hour*. David Franklin told us that he took part
> in a performance of Boughton's opera for television in the
> pioneer days of 1936. 'There were very few TV sets
> around in those days,' he told us, 'and so my wife went to
> watch the production in a special BBC viewing room at
> Broadcasting House. She told me afterwards that I'd been
> singing my head off for twenty minutes or so, when the
> man sitting next to her leaned forward excitedly, clutched
> her arm and cried out, "I think I can see something
> moving!"'

———

In which opera does a mezzo-soprano get pushed into an oven?

> 'Any opera that has the musical instruction "inter
> mezzo",' suggested Denis. Or alternatively – after a little
> prompting from his partner Ian – in *Hansel and Gretel*,
> when the witch is peering into the oven to see if her cakes
> are baked.

———

In which opera does a high priestess have two children by her soldier lover, who then falls in love with one of the virgins in her temple?

Clearly a messy affair all round. After Ian and Denis had struggled with this question for a while, Frank asked them: 'Would you care to borrow David Franklin for two marks?' They did, and eventually came up with the answer: Bellini's *Norma*. (Poor dear.)

———

In another opera, Henry lies to his sister and says that Edgar has been untrue. As a result she agrees to marry Arthur. What happens on the wedding night?

FRANK: If it's opera, they just stand there and sing. Or if you want it in more detail, he makes a little overture, they have a duet *con amore*, and a few months afterwards there's a trio.

The opera is Donizetti's *Lucia di Lammermoor*, from Scott's novel. On the wedding night Lucy stabs Arthur and then dies herself. Edgar returns and follows suit. David's comment: 'Great Scott!'

———

How many girls did Don Giovanni have in Spain?

DENIS: It's very difficult to have any, because when I went to Spain they told me, 'Never put anything to your lips unless you boil it first.' Or (after promptings from Ian) is the answer 1,003?

It is, as in Leporello's *Catalogue song* listing his master's conquests.

———

In Verdi's Aida *the heroine dies in the fourth act beside her lover.
How do they die?*

>   IAN: Permanently.
>   (True. Also they are buried alive.)

How does the Commendatore exact his revenge in Don Giovanni?

>   He invites the Don to dinner, then at the party drags him
>   down to hell. David Franklin, answering this question,
>   was reminded of a Glyndebourne production in its first
>   dress rehearsal. 'Playing the part of the statue, I wore a
>   specially stiffened costume with stone-coloured make-up
>   all over me. I smelt like a polecat. One of the stage hands
>   asked me to go and stand in a corner and close my eyes.
>   I asked why, but he said, "Never mind." Then he dipped
>   a whitewash brush in a pail and started flicking it all over
>   me. "What's that for?" I asked. He replied, "You're
>   supposed to be a statue, aren't you? – Well, that's pigeons.'

In Ariadne and Bluebeard *by Paul Dukas, the heroine is given
seven keys but expressly forbidden to use the seventh. What happens
at that point?*

>   Frank suggested that the seventh key was to the execu-
>   tives' washroom. The heroine, having entered, realized
>   where she was, flushed, and retired in confusion.

'The courtyard of the Kremlin is packed with people on their knees . . .' That comes from the synopsis of Boris Godunov. *Why should thousands of people assume a position on their knees?*

> Because, explained Denis, it was an attempt to curry favour with the Americans by giving a mass impersonation of Al Jolson. Alternatively, but more improbably, they were offering their homage to the new Tsar.

———

' She rides into the heart of the flames, whereupon the river rises in flood and extinguishes the fire. Hagen is drowned; the curse is ended.' Which opera ends like that, Frank?

> *Naughty Marietta?*
> (Wrong. At least I think so, not being too sure of the plot of *Naughty Marietta* myself. But the story sounds to me more like Wagner's *Götterdämmerung*.)

———

In a late scene from La Bohème *the character Schnauard walks off stage carrying something. What is it?*

> IAN: In the stage directions it's a hot water bottle, but I played the part of Schnauard many times and in our productions we always made it a medicine bottle, for the very good reason that a hot water bottle might have got a laugh from the audience where we didn't want one.
>
> In that same scene we had a table centre stage, with on it a small spirit lamp lit by a paraffin flame. On the back of the lamp was a little hook. One evening the singer playing Colline, who was wearing a tail coat with buttons at the back, leaned up against this table and then began a very dignified exit. Unfortunately he had inadvertently hooked the lamp on to his rear. I spotted what had happened and

followed him off very closely in an attempt to prevent the audience seeing. When we got into the wings I said to him, 'What do you think you are? – The 8.20 from Euston?' (*Interesting footnote:* Three months before the premiere of *La Bohème*, his publisher wrote to Puccini, 'If you haven't hit the nail on the head this time I'll change my profession and sell salami!')

———

Where would you find the Nightingale song?

DENIS: In *Iolanthe*. I believe I've heard you sing this, Ian?
IAN WALLACE: Not me.
DENIS: Oh I'm sorry. It must have been *Nellie* Wallace.

———

Who is Mrs Richard Bonynge?

Dame Joan Sutherland, the great Australian operatic soprano whose accompaniments (not unnaturally) are often conducted by Mr Bonynge. John Amis told us of a performance of Handel's *Messiah* at which Miss Sutherland was to sing under the baton of Sir Adrian Boult. Mr Bonynge had written for his wife a splendid cadenza in one of the arias, but had unfortunately neglected to warn Sir Adrian that he had done so. At the end of this glittering cascade of notes at the first rehearsal, Sir Adrian remarked quietly, 'Ah, the Mad Scene from Handel's *Messiah*.'

———

How does Tosca meet her end?

She throws herself from the battlements. Ian told us of one opera house where Tosca's fall was softened, not as is usually the case by a well-placed mattress, but by an inflated balloon-type mattress of the kind that pole-vaulters use. The ample soprano did her dramatic dive . . . only to bounce back again into view.

The hero's initials were B.F. For British audiences they were changed to F.B. Later they were changed back again to B.F. Who was he?

A strange chapter in musical history, this, and not one that seems to be particularly well known. The gentleman in question (if gentleman is the word I want) was Lieutenant Benjamin Franklin Pinkerton of the US Navy. For the first production of *Madame Butterfly* in Britain his name was changed to Sir Francis Blummy Pinkerton. But after the opera's initial failure the new name was dropped, presumably on the assumption that the character would seldom be heard of again.

Quite unashamedly, I put a question to David Franklin that I had culled from his autobiography, Basso Cantante, *which had just been published by Duckworth. The question: Have you ever seen a butler in a harem?*

Yes, replied David, he had. And he recalled how at his beloved Glyndebourne home, the founder, John Christie, had engaged a butler named Childs. Having served dinner to his master's guests, Childs would discreetly withdraw, change into costume and don make-up, and then appear

on stage as a deaf-mute in Mozart's *Entführung*. Christie
didn't believe in wasting a salary!

———

*John – David's successor on our series – worked his way to the
answer of the following rather curious question: Which famous title
role in opera has been sung on records by (respectively) a soprano,
a mezzo-soprano, a contralto, a tenor and a baritone? . . . Though
it wasn't written for any of those voices in the first place.*

The answer is Gluck's Orpheus in *Orfeo and Euridice*
(1762), originally written for a male contralto, Guadagni,
but later recorded by – among others – Marilyn Horne,
Shirley Verrett, Kathleen Ferrier, Nicolai Gedda and
Dietrich Fischer-Dieskau.

———

*Which celebrated English soprano became famous on the French
opera stage, and then changed her name so that Frenchmen would
pronounce it correctly?*

Florrie Forde, according to Denis, who changed her name
to Florrie Citroen. When corrected, and told that it was
Maggie Tate who changed her name to Teyte, he remarked that this change was known in French as *tête à
teyte*. It was a brilliant answer, and it put him two points
ahead.

———

Her real name was Kittl or Krittl. She sang Senta in The Flying
Dutchman; *she was the first Salome, the first Tatiana,
Butterfly, Tess and Minnie. She accepted two and a half thousand
pounds to appear in a film called* The Lion's Bride, *in which she*

sang to eleven lions in a cage and was accompanied by a lady lion-tamer playing the pianoforte. Who was she?

Emmy Destinn (or Destinnova), 1878–1930. Her voice, according to *The Concise Oxford Dictionary of Opera* – which unwittingly has served the *My Music* question-setter well! – was 'of a highly individual timbre'.

A famous opera singer was born in Madrid, gave her singing debut in New York at the age of seven, sang in public for the last time aged seventy-one, and died in Wales. Her name?

Adelina Patti, as David Franklin immediately guessed. Frank then pointed out that Patti and Melba were the two great singers who had items of food named after them. (*Peach Melba* for one.) . . . When I mentioned that Adelina Patti died at her castle in Breconshire, Frank took his cue and named the other dish: *Patti Maison*.

Who composed Russlan and Ludmilla?

While Ian was temporarily labouring under a memory block, David – helpful as ever – said to him: 'If I were you, Ian, I would try Glinka.'
'Stop putting in commercials,' Frank told him.

And finally, as far as opera is concerned: Denis, what can you tell me about Supervia?

'It's an Italian motorway.'

Popera

The panellists of *My Music*, being all on the shady side of fifty (as is their chairman), are not keenly informed rock fans. They do not keep abreast of the times from the point of view of the pop charts, so there is nothing much to be gained by giving them pop records to identify. On the whole they are more at home with popular music of the more middle-of-the-road variety; songs pitched somewhere in period between the Savoy Hotel Orpheans and early Beatles. On the subject of the Lennon and McCartney compositions, Denis Norden once neatly characterized *Eleanor Rigby* as 'the song which caused the boundaries of popular song to be renegotiated': a perceptive comment. And Denis is of course an expert on the musicals of Broadway and Hollywood, just as Frank Muir knows more than most people do about music-hall songs.

But for the most part the contestants remain square and reasonably proud of it.

> DAVID: I never go to the films.
> FRANK: Do you ever go to the pictures?
> DAVID: Not even there. The last time I went to the pictures it was called the Bioscope.

John Amis, magnificently protected from the world of popular music, was once genuinely nonplussed when asked to identify the tune of *How much is that doggie in the window*: he had contrived to live right through the 1950s without once hearing the tune, or at any rate without consciously registering it. John does go to the cinema sometimes, however, and was seen to react when Denis spoke once of 'the unexpurgated story of *The Sound of Music*'.

As for the great solo pop stars, David always insisted on referring to the composer of *Hansel and Gretel* as 'Engelbert Humperdinck the First'. We were all delighted when we learnt that E. Humperdinck the Second got his name as a result of two quite separate inspirations. 'I thought of Engelbert,' said the star. 'It was my manager who thought of Humperdinck.' The more you think about that the better it gets.

For the purposes of this chapter, the heading 'Popera' is taken to include the well-loved light classics, as well as dance- and show-tunes. Saint-Saens' *The Swan*, for example, which Ian Wallace has reason to remember. He was coming round after an anaesthetic in an operating theatre and heard familiar strains issuing from a background music loudspeaker. Recognizing the tune, he asked the sister, 'Couldn't you find something a bit more suitable than *The Dying Swan*?'

Mention of this brought a letter from a Mrs Pam Taylor, writing from an address in Staffordshire. She had come round in a maternity hospital after a very difficult labour, to hear a background tape playing *Who's sorry now?*

But on with the questions and answers, starting with an interesting and little-known fact regarding one of the most famous of all titles in the Broadway canon.

When did The King and I *open on Broadway?*

In 1951. But the title was not new. Browsing through *The Times* dated Wednesday, 4 June 1845 (and doesn't everyone?), I came across an advertisement for the Theatre Royal, Haymarket, which was presenting a new farce. In it, a country bumpkin on a visit to London accidentally met King William the Fourth. The title of the play was *The King and I*. I wonder if Oscar Hammerstein read that copy of *The Times* before I did, or was it just chance?

---

*On the subject of Hammersteiniana, what were the extremes of good
fortune enjoyed professionally by Ezio Fortunatio?*

Having changed his name to Ezio Pinza, he was chosen by
Bruno Walter for *Don Giovanni* and by Rodgers and
Hammerstein for *South Pacific*. Ian, who regards Pinza
as one of his musical heroes, added the curious piece of
information that he – Pinza, not Ian – began his working
life as a racing cyclist.

---

*In another odd piece of Broadway theatrical history, the idea of
making a musical adaptation of a certain play was turned down, in
succession, by Noël Coward, Cole Porter, Yip Harburg, Arthur
Schwartz, and Rodgers and Hammerstein. Clearly the thing was
no good. Who finally accepted the idea?*

Lerner and Loewe: whereupon *Pygmalion* the play became *My Fair Lady* the musical. And a further Broadway
curiosity concerns *The Desert Song*, which was originally
called *Lady Fair*, while Gershwin's *Tell Me More!* (1925)
was actually called *My Fair Lady* during its pre-New
York tryout tour.

---

*Over the years Rodgers and Hammerstein had some fairly mixed
receptions from the press. One critic said that* The Sound of Music
*was 'for people who find James Barrie pretty rough stuff'. But the
tersest review came, predictably, from Kenneth Tynan, who called
one of their musicals* A World of Woozy Song. *Which musical was
that?*

Easy of course: *Flower Drum Song*. But it reminded Frank
of another crushing Ken Tynan review, in which he said
that *The Sound of Music* 'will suit all ages from 13 to 14'.

What was the first music heard on the moon?

> *Lava come back to me,* suggested Frank, as the audience erupted. It was in fact *The Army Air Corps song,* played on tape, as Apollo 15 left the moon at the end of July 1971.

———

Which film first featured the song Baby it's cold outside?

> It was *Neptune's Daughter,* with Esther Williams, Red Skelton, Betty Garrett, Keenan Wynn and Ricardo Montalban. Frank described Esther Williams as 'a sort of wet Doris Day'.

———

Who conducted Music from the Movies *for radio?*

> Louis Levy. John Amis recalled that Levy was a highly professional studio conductor, much admired and well liked, but not perhaps the most scholarly of men. Once on a recording session the orchestra was playing rather quietly when Louis Levy tapped his baton against the conductor's stand and called out, 'Come on, chaps, let's have a bit more noise!' The leader protested. 'Mr Levy, it says on the music *morendo.*' And Levy replied, 'Well all right but let's have more of it, boys. Don't just let it die away!'

———

It opened in 1910 with Nellie Wallace. The original prospectus read, 'In the great Palm Court, one thousand persons can be comfortably served with tea, while a ladies' orchestra plays daily.' By 1928 the main hall had become a cinema, but live entertainment was re-established there in 1932 with a special comedy week. What is the building, and what was that special week?

The building is the London Palladium. The special week was the first Crazy Week (1932) with the Crazy Gang.

Denis had reason to remember that Crazy Week, Not only was he there; it was little Denis's first ever visit to the theatre. His father and mother took him as a special treat.

But the 'crazy' idea was new, and unknown to the audience the members of the Crazy Gang had moved down into the auditorium and taken the place of the ushers checking the tickets as the audience filed in. When little Denis arrived with Mr and Mrs Norden senior, Bud Flanagan rejected their tickets loudly, calling out, 'We don't want your sort here. Out!'

'I was desolate,' said Denis. 'I thought that was what happened at the theatre.'

Who made Khachaturian's Sabre Dance *suddenly famous?*

I had in mind the Andrews Sisters. But Frank suggested that the *Sabre Dance* was famous for having been introduced by a Russian dancer called 'No-toes Petrov'.

Who was 'Banjo Eyes'?

Eddie Cantor. A mention of his 1933 film *Roman Scandals* reminded Ian of an exchange of dialogue from that or perhaps some similar film, in which one camel turned to another and said, 'When I look at these human beings, I'm glad I'm a camel.' And the other replied, '*I'm* glad you're a camel, too, Myrtle.'

Somehow the name seems right. And talking of names –

Who was Ish Kabibble?

Not a man to trifle with, that's for sure. He was in fact the featured comedian with Kay Kayser's Band in several Hollywood musical films of the 1930s and 40s. A member of the trumpet section in his more musical moments, he was notable for his straight hair-fringe. In some ways he anticipated the comedy style of Jerry Lewis.

Denis recalled a memorable remark made by Kay Kayser: 'You can make a musician out of a gentleman, but you can never make a gentleman out of a musician.'

———

In the words of a song: when I'm dancing with the wrong person I get blurred vision. Why?

Frank suggested tight pumps. Then David Franklin got it: *I'm dancing with tears in my eyes ('cos the girl in my arms isn't you).*

———

Who wrote the words of the song Trees?

Frank knew: it was a gentleman called Joyce Kilmer – Alfred Joyce Kilmer – who died during the First World War. Somewhere in America, it transpires, there is a memorial to the man who wrote this touching song lyric about trees. Unfortunately a few years ago the County Commissioners found it necessary to cut down two-thirds of the trees around the monument so that passers-by could read the inscription!

———

Who composed the famous theme for the film Exodus?

DENIS: This was Ernest Gold. The film, by the way, ran for four and a half hours, which is a long time, even if you're Jewish. It's reported that after sitting through two hours of it, Frankie Vaughan plucked at an usherette's sleeve and said, 'Let my people go.'

———

What was the Castle Walk?

It was a dance similar to the one-step, invented by Vernon and Irene Castle during the First World War. But that sort of answer isn't good enough for Frank Muir. 'The Castle Walk,' said Frank, 'stems from medieval times. It was a very stiff-legged affair, due to the fact that people used to spend a lot of their time sitting on damp castle walls. Those ancient piles gave their names to many things . . .'

———

Can you name the Seven Dwarfs in the Disney film?

DENIS: Sneezy, Dozy, Wheezy, Verdi, Athos, Porthos and Aramis.

———

Can you complete the 1921 song line 'They needed a songbird in heaven . . .'?

David had heard of this one, and gave the full correct, revolting title: 'They needed a songbird in heaven, so God took Caruso away'. David told us that he once saw an

In Memoriam advertisement in a Midlands paper which
read:

> *The silver trumpets sounded,*
> *The angels whispered 'Come';*
> *They opened wide the pearly gates*
> *And in walked Mum.*

Ian added a Scots tribute:

> *We were eleven in the family,*
> *Quite a quiverful.*
> *We left Scotland*
> *And went to Liverpool.*
> *But now Annie has gone to see God,*
> *Killed by a bus in the Paisley Road.*

We have had much fun over the years with song titles,
especially when recalling old forgotten songs with ingenious
names or lyrics. How nice it was to be reminded of Dan Leno's
song *Young men taken in and done for*; the unanswerable *Why
build a wall round a graveyard, when nobody wants to get in?*, and
the pun that for sheer cheek beat many of the *My Music* answers:
You can't keep a horse in a lighthouse, neigh, neigh, neigh. A
mention too for Wilkie Bard's *She cost me seven and sixpence, I
wish I'd bought a dog.*

The public's determination in asking for songs under the
wrong titles has long delighted musicians who are on the re-
ceiving end of requests. (I have gone into this more deeply in my
autobiography, *Musician at Large*.) The best known of these
mistaken titles is *You are the one*, when what the listener wants
to hear is *Night and day*. And that song is closely followed in
popularity by *I get too hungry*, which turns out to be *The lady is
a tramp*.

This subject brought a pleasing anecdote from a listener in
Glasgow, Gordon Ritchie, who was playing the piano in a
restaurant there when a waitress came up to him and passed on a
request from one of the customers. 'He says will you play *False
teeth*?' Not being able to remember any tune with such an unlikely title, Mr Ritchie went over to the customer's table. 'Ex-

cuse me, was it you that wanted me to play *False teeth*?' he asked. 'No it was not,' snapped the diner. 'Not *False teeth* – *Valse triste*!'

———

What is the origin of the word juke *in* Juke Box?

Juke is the southern American name for an inn. It derives originally from Chaucerian English: *jowken*, to rest or sleep.

Frank had another idea. He told us that *juke* was an old Scots word meaning to dodge or weave (similar, he said, to the word jink). So a *juke-box* is something to dodge or avoid.

He could be right.

Ops

So ends an-other e-di-tion of   'My Music'—

Who composed Rustle of Spring?

    FRANK: I don't know.
    DAVID: Try Sinding.
    FRANK: I can't sind.

When confronted with orchestral and instrumental records our panellists tend to enjoy the music so much that they forget to answer the questions. But many good things have resulted from works like the one by Tchaikovsky which John likes to call *The Crutknacker Suite.* Sometimes the answers are admirably terse, as when Denis Norden was asked about a Gustav Holst score:

Who was The Perfect Fool?

    DENIS: He was an American university professor who worked on a cure for nymphomania.

Or when I asked Frank:

What are described as Little Russian and Pathetic?

    FRANK: Virgin Sturgeon.

The only thing about being the question-setter and chairman is that I always have to provide the correct answers, no matter how tedious they are in comparison with what has been proposed by the team members. In this case I had to put it on record that the Little Russian and the Pathetic were symphonies by Tchaikovsky, and I played a rather sombre bit of the latter on my piano as a bonus. Whereupon Denis was visibly disturbed, and said 'Oh, I shall have to take Teddy to bed tonight.'

What do orchestral musicians call The egg-timer?

Mozart's overture to *The Marriage of Figaro*, because with a bit of a dash the orchestra can manage to get through the piece in the time it takes to boil an egg.

The overture is fast-moving; it should also be begun very quietly, which is not always easy when the string players' bows are moving rapidly up and down in a flurry of quavers. David recalled for us a charming story of how the conductor Fritz Busch had raised his baton at a rehearsal, then stopped, and lowered it again before a single note had been played. 'You see, gentlemen,' he said triumphantly. 'Already it is too loud!'

———

What does Intermezzo *mean, and why is it a little unexpected that* Cavalleria Rusticana *should have one?*

Cav (as professional musicians call it), is a one-act opera, so its famous *Intermezzo* – meaning 'half-way through' – could hardly occupy its usual place between acts. It occurs, in fact, in the middle of the act while the stage remains empty. Its composer, Mascagni, made *Cav* a one-act opera for the excellent reason that he had entered it for a one-act opera competition. With more than one act it would simply not have been eligible!

This question reminded Ian of the opera house at Parma in Italy, where he claimed that the shortest-ever performance took place of *Cav*'s usual partner, *Pag* (*Pagliacci*).

The opera begins with a baritone who comes on to deliver the Prologue and sings, in Italian of course, the two introductory words 'May I?' On this occasion the entire audience rose as one man and shouted back 'No!'

———

*Haydn's 96th Symphony has long been known as 'The Miracle'.
Why?*

> Because (said Denis) he told his wife, 'I've written 95
> Symphonies already, and if I finish this one it'll be a
> miracle.'
>
> Nearly right, though scholars have now decided that
> the Miracle Symphony was actually No. 102, so in Denis's
> reply, for 95 read 101. At the first performance of the
> symphony in question a huge chandelier crashed to the
> floor of the hall. However, the audience had already
> crowded round Haydn on the platform in order to con-
> gratulate him, so by a miracle no one was hurt. Moral:
> Always go up and thank a performer after his show!

---

*A contemporary critic described a work as resembling 'the march of
men, the sounding of the charge, the thundering of the onset, the
groans of the wounded and the hellish roar of war'. Which work?*

> Frank's suggestion – *Salad Days* – proved to be less than
> correct. It was Haydn's Military Symphony, No. 100 in
> G major. (Or have the experts renumbered that too?)

---

*What will you find at the Villa Borghese, on the Appian Way, and
near a catacomb?*

> In these tourist days, rather a lot of chewing gum, I
> shouldn't wonder. But the correct musical answer is in
> the various movements of Respighi's orchestral suite *The
> Pines of Rome*.

Can you give me an example of chamber music?

> DAVID: How about Handel's Music for the Royal
> Waterworks?

In France and Germany, they know the tune as Cutlets. *Borodin,
Rimsky-Korsakov and Liszt wrote variations on it. What do we
call it?*

> We call it *Chopsticks*, as Denis knew. He also gave us an
> interesting new piece of international intelligence: in
> China, *Chopsticks* is known as *Knife and fork*.

---

*The composer said of it, 'It will be very loud and noisy. I wrote it
without any warm feelings of love, so it will probably be of no
artistic worth.' Which piece of music was that?*

> Tchaikovsky's *1812 Overture*. A supporter of ours, who
> works in the stores department of the Greater London
> Council, was delighted to see an official-looking library
> order which requested the supply of '1 Overture, 18 × 12'.
> Another fan of the programme wrote to me from Ret-
> ford with a delicious story about Vic Oliver, who one
> morning bumped into a musician he had known in his
> younger days. 'How are you getting on?' inquired Vic.
> 'Fine,' his friend replied. 'I'm running a little orchestra:
> there are five of us. Do come next Saturday – we're doing
> Beethoven's Fifth Symphony.'
> Vic Oliver thought quickly. 'I'm sorry,' he said, 'I'm
> working this Saturday.'
> 'All the better!' cried his acquaintance excitedly.
> 'Come the following Saturday – we're doing *1812*!'

What is a two-part invention?

Not, as Denis suggested, Shakespeare's *Henry the Fourth*, but a short contrapuntal piece for two parts or 'voices'.

Which American avant-garde composer wrote a work consisting of 4 minutes 33 seconds of total silence?

John Cage. Stravinsky observed that he was looking forward to 'a full-length work by the same composer'.

Who composed the RAF March Past?

This question, posed by 1334498 Sergeant Race S., brought an all-present-and-correct answer from 1615359 LAC Norden D. 'It was Sir Walford Davies, wasn't it, Steve?' Right. It also served to remind Denis of the immortal couplet:

> *Heart of oak are our men,*
> *Head of oak are our officers.*

And after a certain amount of rather tedious and bitter reminiscence on both our parts, Denis dredged up the memory of a drill sergeant saying to him, through gritted teeth: 'If you drop your rifle this time, *faint*!'

For further RAF memories – yes, you've guessed it – see my autobiography.

Who composed a colourful Cuban Overture?

Probably any unpronouncable Cuban composer, and I was lucky not to be told so. The composer I had in mind

was George Gershwin in 1932. Having played to the
panel a few bars of the recording conducted by Sir Adrian
Boult, I admitted to having at first thought that Gershwin's music was a strange choice for Boult. Then I
reflected on the fact that composer and conductor were
precisely of the same generation, Gershwin having been
born in 1898 and Boult in 1899. It merely happened that
one of them enjoyed a much longer life than the other.

John underlined the wide range of Sir Adrian's musical
interests, and recalled that after conducting a performance of *The Dance of the Seven Veils* from *Salome* the
old gentleman was heard to remark under his breath,
'Nasty, urge-y music.'

---

*At the first performance of Beethoven's Violin Concerto what
happened between the 1st and 2nd movements?*

Incredibly, the soloist – Clement – played an Interlude, a
sort of cabaret spot, including a special piece which called
for the violin to be held upside down!

It is reported, I hope truthfully, that when Mrs Yehudi
Menuhin is present at one of her husband's performances
of the Beethoven Violin Concerto, she sings to herself, as
he reaches the haven of the final jaunty theme: 'Thank
God it's over, thank God it's over, it's over, it's over, it's
over at last . . .'

True or false, I don't know. But I do know that the
former doorman at a famous recording studio in Abbey
Road, London, once inquired genially, 'Is that Yehudi
Moynihan coming in this morning?'

Why is Beethoven's overture called Leonora No. 3?

Because it was one of three attempts at an overture of that name – which is the sort of answer I usually get from Denis or Frank, but happened to be true anyway.

Denis has a gloss to add. He told us that Beethoven, having finished his overture, decided to dedicate it to his girl friend, and rang her up to say that he was bringing the score round to her flat. 'Not tonight, Ludwig,' she replied, 'I've got to wash my hair. But if you call round you can leave the music with the porter. Just put my name and flat number on it . . .'

———

What is the popular title for the principal theme of Bach's Cantata No. 208?

Sheep may safely graze. Of all the many stories sent in by kind listeners and viewers to *My Music*, among the most charming was the one that came from a lady in Sussex. Driving through a picturesque village one day she heard the sound of that tune being played in the village church. 'What's the occasion?' she asked. 'It's a funeral,' she was told, as the strains of *Sheep may safely graze* wafted through the windows. 'Whose funeral?' 'Our butcher's.'

Listeners' and viewers' stories vary from the truthful and new to the apocryphal and (let's be honest) sometimes rather well known. Just in case it isn't universally known, let me recall the newspaper account of various alterations and improvements that had been made in the York Minster organ; a report which ended with the unforgettable words: 'As a result of these modifications, the organist can now change his combinations without leaving his seat.'

———

What was the origin of the music used in the ballet Love in Bath?

> DENIS: *Land of soap and glory.* Or possibly *Loofah come back to me.*
> FRANK: It was a plug number, anyway.
>
> (For the record – and a very enjoyable record too, I remember – it was Sir Thomas Beecham who used various themes by Handel to construct his ballet score.)

What is the basic difference between playing the flute and playing the recorder?

> The flute is held transversely to the mouth; the recorder points forwards. That, at any rate, is my answer, though I feel sure it could be expressed more elegantly. In any case, everyone knows the answer.
> Everyone except Frank. According to him, the difference is more picturesque. If you are standing with your right shoulder up against a wall, he maintains, you can play the recorder but you can't play the flute. That is the difference.
> Denis added that the extraordinary thing to him about flute players is how they manage to play the instrument at all without constantly raising their eyebrows. (At that point a lady flute player who happened to be in the audience called out to us that she *always* raised her eyebrows while playing, which just goes to show how perceptive Denis is on technical matters.)

Which is the largest bell in Britain?

> None of my contestants knew, though I am sure many readers do. It is Great Paul in St Paul's Cathedral. It

weighs over sixteen tons (where have I heard that figure before?) and is tolled, as opposed to being struck like Big Ben.

———

Watching a symphony orchestra in action, one sometimes sees the tympanist lean down and place his head close to one of his drums. What is he doing?

(Why do I ask questions like this?) 'Having a swift gin,' replied Frank instantly. 'Or in the case of a kettle drum, a cup of tea.' He went on to explain that the man is actually screwing and unscrewing the faucets in order to change the pitch, as he wants to hear what he is doing. The other musicians are battling away as loudly as possible in order to catch him out.

———

The marvels to be admired and enjoyed at Prince Esterhazy's palace, we are told, included an armchair that played the flute whenever anybody sat on it. The interesting question arises: which tune did it play?

We don't know. (My guess would be *Check to cheek*.) Denis remarked that previously he had only heard of people playing by ear, but supposed the tune was that old American favourite *Hallelujah, I'm a bum.*

———

Can you recall what the good Doctor Johnson said of a violinist's performance?

He had been told that it was 'a very difficult piece'. Doctor Johnson replied, 'Difficult, do you call it, sir? I wish it were impossible.'

It was futile to think that this question would cause Frank the slightest brow-furrowing, since he is highly knowledgeable on matters of eighteenth-century literature. *The Frank Muir Book* is full of delicious quotations from that wonderful age: the only century apart from ours in which I – or Frank either, I imagine – would care to have lived. In his perpetual vendetta against all quizmasters, including me, Frank once described me as 'Remote, unfriended, melancholy, slow', and I didn't mind a bit, recognizing the source.

Friends used to greet a certain Russian composer with the words: 'How are you? Not too well, I hope?' Who was he, and why did they say that?

He was Borodin. As an amateur, part-time composer he could only write music in what little leisure his job as a director of chemistry allowed him. Whenever he had a cold he stayed away from work and did some composing, to the delight of his friends and admirers.

Who wrote, 'A poet past thirty-five seems a trifle obscene; as if one had encountered a greying man who still played the Chopin waltzes'?

H. L. Mencken was the rather cruel author of that remark. (Cruel, because I too am greying, if not more so, and would like to feel that I can still get away with the odd Chopin waltz, or even two in the right situation.) Mencken also wrote, 'Poetry is a comforting piece of fiction set to more or less lascivious music.' And mention of that splendid American reminded Denis of Mencken's charming epitaph which he wrote for himself: 'If after I depart this vale you remember me and have thought to please my ghost, forgive some sinner and wink your eye at a homely girl.'

Finally Frank recalled Mencken's crisp 'There are two sorts of music: German and bad.'

Who was Enesco?

George Enesco (1881–1955), Romanian composer and conductor, and violin teacher of Menuhin. More to the point, in *My Music*'s terms, Enesco was John Amis's nomination as the most remarkable musician he had ever met. He then told a story which he had recently heard from Artur Rubinstein.

Enesco was prevailed upon to repay an old personal debt by taking on as a violin pupil the somewhat un-talented son of a friend. When it became necessary for the young man to give a debut recital, Enesco even allowed himself to be talked into accompanying him at the piano.

On the evening of the recital Enesco, realizing at the last moment that he would need a page-turner, persuaded his friend, Alfred Cortot, the distinguished pianist, to come up out of the audience and assist him. The following morning a review appeared in *Figaro*, which read: 'A curious recital took place last night at the Salle Gaveau. The man who was turning the pages should by rights have been playing the piano. The man who was playing the piano ought to have been playing the violin. And the violinist ought really to have been turning the pages . . .'

Truly It Has Been Said

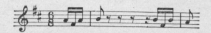

A friend of mine once remarked at a Chopin recital: 'I don't think much of that Impromptu he just played, do you? It sounded as though he was making it up as he went along.'

The nice thing about that was that it was said quite seriously. Other quotable remarks are less innocent, for example Bernard Shaw's exchange with a reporter on his return from a visit to Hollywood.

> REPORTER: How did it go in Hollywood, Mr Shaw?
> G.B.S.: The trouble was, gentlemen, that Mr Goldwyn was interested in art, and I was interested in money.

For myself, I enjoy most the 'how true' line, like Logan Pearsall Smith's confession, 'How often my soul visits the National Gallery, and how seldom I go there myself.' Or for that matter, the xenophobic remark quoted by John in one of our programmes, after some Swiss music had been briefly discussed: 'If the Swiss had made their own mountains they would have been very much flatter.'

But let me put some quotable quotes in question-and-answer form:

Who said, 'Beware of criticizing royal music. You never know who wrote it'?

Brahms.

Who do you think said, 'My music is best understood by children and animals'?

> DENIS: The man who said that was the producer of *My Music*. (Right. Or failing him, Igor Stravinsky.)

———

What did Siegfried Wagner say of Hansel and Gretel?

> He called it 'the most important opera since *Parsifal*'. Upon which the critic Hanslick commented: 'An irritating pronouncement. And the worst of it is that it's true!'

———

Who said 'I am disposed towards harmony, but organically I am incapable of a tune'?

> Charles Lamb. (Though John Amis suggested Schoenberg!)

———

Where do you find the line 'Frustrate their knavish tricks'?

> In the National Anthem: 'Scatter her enemies and make them fall, confound their politics, frustrate their knavish tricks, on thee our hopes we fix . . .'
> This quotation reminded Denis of a remark made somewhere by Evelyn Waugh, who said that 'only schoolchildren and spies know the second verse of the National Anthem'.
> This in turn reminded me of the story that Frenchmen like to tell one another, of a sentry on guard duty who called, 'Who goes there?'

'A Frenchman,' came the reply.

'Prove it. Sing the second verse of *La Marseillaise*.'

'I can't remember it.'

'Pass, Frenchman.'

On the subject of that magnificent national song, the stirring qualities of *La Marseillaise* were so powerful that one French general in difficulties is reported to have demanded either 10,000 men or a few copies of the song. As for the name itself, it was the popularity of the song with the soldiers of Marseilles, marching on Paris in 1792, that gave it its name.

———

Arnold Bennett went to see a highly successful show, and so disliked it that he summed it up in a crisp line or two in his diary: 'Music even less charming than I expected. Plot all about drinking, whoring and money. Names of tarts on the lips of characters all the time . . .' What dreadful piece of pornography brought on such a description?

The Merry Widow. The 'names of tarts on the lips of characters' must have been Danilo's delightful *I'm going to Maxim's*.

———

What did Queen Victoria say when she had been to see Aida?

According to Ian she said, 'We are not amused', or at best, 'Jolly good show!' But according to the reference books she said, '*Proper* soldiers should be used', since when many productions have used members of the Brigade of Guards. They are indeed more soldierly than members of Equity, and presumably cheaper too.

———

A great composer on a visit to England heard the Hallelujah chorus
*performed in Westminster Abbey, rose to his feet weeping and made
a famous remark. What was the famous remark?*

> FRANK: Sssh!
> Maybe so. But he – Haydn – also said, of Handel:
> 'He is the master of us all.'

What was Richard Strauss's advice to young conductors?

> 'Never look encouragingly at the brass.'

------

*Which composer wrote to another composer, 'Great Chief, receive
my tomahawk!' – and what did he enclose?*

> Denis said that his mind was racing through the names of
> the many Red Indian composers. Could it perhaps have
> been the composer of *Sweet Sioux*?
> It could not. It could, on the other hand, have been
> Hector Berlioz, exchanging conductors' batons with
> Mendelssohn. The actual baton he sent is in the Paris
> Conservatoire to this day.

A postscript to these quotable musical quotes, as quoted by John
Amis on the subject of his former employer Sir Thomas
Beecham. (He was Beecham's concerts manager for a while):

> SOMEONE TO BEECHAM: Have you ever conducted any
> Stockhausen?
> BEECHAM: No, but I once trod in some.

The Conductor is Always Right

Sir Thomas Beecham once remarked, 'So far as the public is concerned, there are only two requisites for a good performance: that the orchestra should start together and finish together. The public does not give a damn what goes on in between.'

Beecham made good music and good copy in almost equal proportions. Ian recalled for us how Sir Thomas once took the violinist Jean Pougnet to a provincial concert where the great man had been engaged to conduct a rather poor orchestra. After a chaotic start the terrified musicians fell into some semblance of step with their lordly conductor. Throughout the whole lash-up, Sir Thomas had been beating away, apparently unconcerned. Now he leaned down towards his leader and said quietly, 'Don't look now, Mr Pougnet, but I believe we're being followed.'

Two Tommy fans, Harold Atkins and Archie Newman, gathered together that and many other gems for their book *Beecham Stories*. They could hardly fail to report the telephone conversation in a New York hotel room:

'This is Sir Thomas Beecham. Who is speaking?'

'Oh Sir Tarmas, ah yairm the secretary of the N'York Brainch of the English-speaking Union.'

'I don't believe it.'

One story always leads to another, and Denis found himself reminded of a party in trendy San Francisco attended by a friend of his. Trying to make small talk with a weird-looking apparition in beard, kaftan and beads, he inquired what the young man did for a living. 'Like man, my bag is, I'm into teaching English,' was the reply.

But we digress. (Often.) Back to those orchestral conductors, and to questions about them.

In the year 1900, Leopold Antoni Stokowski got the job of organist at the church of St James, Piccadilly in London. What did he decide to call himself?

> Stokes. Later, as a conductor in America, he changed his name back to Stokowski, having been born in London of Polish descent. For many years the idea persisted that he had been born 'Stokes' and affected the foreign-sounding variation of 'Stokowski' in order to impress.

Not a bit of it. A kind listener to *My Music* heard us on the subject of Stokowski *v*. Stokes and sent me a photostat of the maestro's birth certificate, showing conclusively that he was registered at All Souls in the London parish of Marylebone on 1 June 1882, having been born at 13 Upper Marylebone Street on 18 April, the son of Kopernik Stokowski (cabinet maker) and Annie Stokowski (formerly Moore).

London-born or not, Stokowski maintained a somewhat fractured English accent until his dying day. This was probably what gave rise to the nicest – and perhaps the most improbable – story about him. On one of his returns to London to conduct, he was met at Waterloo station by a representative of the orchestra's management. In the taxi they had exchanged a few words across what seemed to be an insurmountable language barrier. Then as the cab swung into Parliament Square, Stokowski pointed up towards Big Ben. 'How you call big clock?' he inquired affably.

Equally as disputed as the details of Stokowski's birth is the location of Sir Malcolm Sargent's birthplace. Which leads to the straightforward question: where was Sargent born?

Ninety-nine people out of a hundred will reply 'in Stamford, Lincolnshire', and they are supported by nine out of ten reference books. But a lady named Hall, writing to me from Ashford in Kent, enclosed a colour photograph of a plaque on a house in Beaver Road there, which reads, quite clearly: 'Sir Malcolm

Sargent, the distinguished conductor was born here, 29th April, 1895.' It is correct: his mother was visiting Ashford when he was born, though their home was in Stamford.

Asked about Sir Malcolm, Denis told us 'I sang under him once – in front of my television set.' Actually, the number of people who did sing under Sir Malcolm's inspiring baton must have run literally into hundreds of thousands. I have yet to meet a Welshman who did not sing *Messiah* under him. Equally most of them also boozed with Dylan Thomas and hewed the living rock with Aneurin Bevan, but that's another story (and an extremely long one). Sir Malcolm used to say that the dream of every Welsh tenor was eventually to go through the Pearly Gates and join the heavenly male voice choir, which he would find on arrival consisted of a thousand basses and one tenor – himself. At the first rehearsal, St Peter would start them off, then stop the choir, turn to the newly-arrived tenor and say, 'Mr Jones, a little less voice, if you please.'

Can you think of an anagram of Knappertsbusch?

Of course not. But mention of him does trigger off a story from John, about how Knappertsbusch once went to conduct a distinctly inferior orchestra at Bochum in the Ruhr. After the concert, an enthusiastic chairman of the orchestral board engaged him in conversation. 'Tell me, Maestro, when was the last time you conducted the Bochum Symphony Orchestra?'

'Tonight,' he replied.

Bad performances are the mainstay of many conductor stories. Ian recalled an un-named Italian conductor who was so dismayed by the awful piccolo player in an orchestra that he walked

over to him while the music was going on, quietly took the
instrument from his hand and slipped it into the player's pocket.

Ian is not above telling a story against himself. Singing under
Stanford Robinson for the first time in a studio performance of
Vaughan Williams's *Hugh the Drover*, Ian found himself so
nervous that, as he put it, 'I was half conducting with my right
hand as I sang. To my horror, Robbie stopped the orchestra and
called out to me: "Mr Wallace, you must not conduct with your
right hand. I don't know whether to follow your beat or mine.
And it couldn't matter less, anyway, because you're not following either!"'

Ian has naturally had more experience of conductors at work
than any of us. He told us – though not from his own experience
– about a conductor of fiery Italian temperament who was to
conduct an amateur orchestra somewhere in the southern half
of his country. The horn player was a very placid man but his
playing was somewhat substandard, and in order to keep the
conductor off his neck the organizer had arranged a small
deception. 'Maestro,' he said, 'the horn player: he is a very
violent man. He carries a knife. Do not offend him.'

Came the first rehearsal and the horn player made a false
entry, and on the wrong note as well. The conductor was wary.
'Not quite perfect,' he said. 'We start again.' A second time and
a third were no better. Eventually, after the fourth calamitous
entry the conductor's patience snapped. Rushing over to the
horn section and tugging open his shirt, he held his breast
towards the startled horn player. 'Kill me!' he cried. 'Kill me!
But go!'

A sad story perhaps. Though not as sad as that of the American cellist, who made a false entry during a Fritz Reiner concert,
coming in loudly during an otherwise silent bar. After the concert he was sent for by the conductor and abruptly sacked. But
the poor cellist pleaded for his job. 'Herr Reiner,' he said, 'it
was only a tiny mistake.' The conductor was adamant. 'It's not
the fact that you came in wrong,' he said. 'Anybody can do that.
No, it's your playing. None of us had ever heard you before!'

I contributed a story told to me by the horn player Alan Civil,
who in turn had heard it from the great cellist Rostropovich,

about his father. Rostropovich Senior, also a musician, was once playing in a radio broadcast of the Tchaikovsky 6th Symphony in a Moscow studio, when suddenly all the lights went out, plunging the place into complete darkness. The orchestra faltered on for a second or two, then gathered confidence, and – good Russians to a man – completed the symphony in darkness.

Soon after the last chord died away, the lights went on again. The musicians fell to congratulating one another . . . Until they noticed the conductor, sitting on his podium with his head in his hands. Poor man – he had discovered that they could do without him.

One of the best conductor stories came from John, when we sat on the stage of Cheltenham Town Hall, as part of the Cheltenham International Festival of Music; one of our rare visits outside our 'home' at the Commonwealth Institute. According to John, Sir Adrian Boult was one afternoon on that very same Cheltenham stage, conducting a programme of newly-composed and somewhat weird contemporary music, one of the items being a work by the composer X.

The rehearsal had been going for some time when Mr X himself arrived, sat in the stalls, and listened to the music, showing increasing signs of restlessness and irritation. In the end he stood up.

'Sir Adrian,' he called out, 'Sir Adrian, could you *please* take it a little quicker?'

Sir Adrian Boult peered down into the stalls. 'Ah, Mr X,' he said. 'Yes, certainly we can take it quicker if you wish. But you do realize that we haven't come to your piece yet, don't you?'

Again from John came a story about Ansermet, the Swiss conductor, who (as John reminded us) had a magnificent command over music but rather less over the English language. To a tiresome concerto soloist who repeatedly complained about the tempos at rehearsal, he called out in final desperation: 'Don't spoke! Don't spoke! If you didn't like it, you went!'

And the same conductor, to an orchestra which had been rather persistently playful in rehearsal: 'Look, a joke, then and now, yes very. But always, by God, never!'

Once a Pun a Time

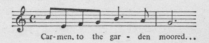

Car-men, to the gar - den moored...

'A man who would make so vile a pun would not scruple to pick a pocket.'

The Gentleman's Magazine (1781)

One of our listeners perpetrated the worst pun in musical history when he wrote, 'Bach and the world Bachs with you; Offenbach, and you Barcarolle.' After that, anything was a relief, even my anonymous correspondent's translation of *Questa o quella* as 'I am looking for a seasick pill'.

My own belief is that in order to enjoy an ingenious pun one has only to stop groaning like a schoolboy and enjoy the thing like a man. Puns are grossly underrated, perhaps deliberately, by people whose command of the language is not sufficiently quick to produce one the instant an opportunity presents itself.

Nobody could accuse Messrs Muir, Norden, Wallace, Franklin and Amis of being slow to make a pun – as the following paragraphs testify.

A Mr Cunningham wrote from East Grinstead to point out how many animals' names seem to occur in musical titles: Kitten on the keys, Sheep may safely graze *and so on. Any newly invented ones, he wondered?*

He did not have to wonder for long. Impromptu (of course) Frank offered *Unforget a bull.* Ian suggested Irving Berlin's *Big horse, I love you.* Denis came up with the masterly *Did chihuahua see a dream walking?* Mr Cunningham's own treble contender – though not impromptu, presumably – was the splendid *Ewe otter bee in pictures*.

It seems somehow satisfactory when professional people have really apt names, like Mr Bun the Baker in Happy Families. Passing a strip club near Piccadilly Circus I noticed a poster advertising the star of the show and was delighted to see that her name was Misty Mina.

How about an apt name for a musician?

Denis worked his way towards three ladies' names, one operatic, the other two from the more popular repertoire: Barbara Seville, Bertha D. Bluse, and Sonia Papermoon.

My dentist has installed stereophonic earphones in his surgery so that we patients can listen to calming music while being drilled or scraped. What would be a good piece of music for a dentist to avoid playing to his patient?

Frank had two suggestions. One was the line from Elgar's famous patriotic song that goes 'Wider still and wider . . .' The other possibility, Frank thought, was the hymn line 'Change and decay in all around I see . . ' With time to brood on it in advance, I had decided that the tunes I would least like to hear while in the dentist's chair were *I'll never smile again* and *This'll make you whistle*.

Having found some suitable tunes for my musically-minded dentist to play to his patients – or rather, unsuitable tunes – we turned our attention next to maternity hospitals. Well-chosen background music can have a calming effect on expectant mothers (and let us not forget expectant fathers too). But what should the management avoid playing in a maternity hospital?

Possibly because I had just been glancing through a collection of Charles Addams cartoons, I was able to start the ball rolling with *Two heads are better than one*. Ian thought an expectant father would be concerned if he were to hear *June is busting out all over*. Denis wondered if an April mother might respond to *The things we did last summer*. Frank's first suggestion was *Baby, it's cold outside*, but he later withdrew that suggestion in favour of the least desirable of all Maternity Home cautionary tales, *Mary had a little lamb*.

What would be a good tune to play as the haggis is being brought ceremonially to the table at a Scots banquet?

Ian, our resident Scot of that ilk, suggested *Someday my mince will come*. In the end he settled for *When my sheep comes in*.

British Airways passengers crossing the great oceans and continents of the world were for many years offered a programme of taped classical music, introduced by the calm, reassuring voice of – I have to admit it – Steve Race. As I explained to the panel, we tried to make the selections from a wide range of music, but there were some titles it was thought best to avoid. After all, passengers were far from home and loved ones, encapsulated thousands of feet up in the air, and inclined to be highly nervous. Which particular pieces of music ought we to be at pains to avoid?

DENIS: I don't know about British Airways flights, but on entering an American airliner it might be nice if one didn't hear the old film song that began 'How would you like to spend an evening in Havana . . . ?'

DAVID: I have two suggestions. If it were me, I'd rather not hear *O for the wings of a dove*, or the song from *Porgy and Bess*, *O Lord, I'm on my way*.

We all agreed in the end that it would be best to avoid *That old black magic*, with its line 'Down and down I go, round and round I go, in a spin . . .'

———

Put yourselves in an imaginary situation. You are a young man, engaged to a girl whom frankly you no longer want. Being a nice sort of person, you invite her out to dinner in order to break it to her that the whole thing is off. Suitably anaesthetized by good food and good wine, you are just coming round to announcing to her the fateful decision, when the resident band begins to play. To your horror, you realize that they are playing . . . What?

Ian thought that one unfortunate choice at that moment would be a selection from *Bless the Bride*, especially if the band started off with *This is my lovely day*. But Denis won the hand: he nominated Irving Berlin's song called *After you've got what you want you don't want it*.

———

A supporter of our programme living in Hampstead – Colin Smith by name – wanted to know which songs might figure in an LP called *Songs for Swinging Fishmongers*.

Mr Smith himself suggested *Salmon chanted evening* (presumably fished out of the South Pacific). Frank excelled himself with a triple pun: *Whale kipper whelk-ome in the hillsides*. And our TV producer, Duggie Hespe, worked out an ingenious double: *Carmina Piranha*, by Carl Orfe.

———

Speaking as someone who is addicted to cheese, I was delighted to find that there is an official public-relations organization called The Cheese Board. Can you think of a suitable signature tune for the cheese industry?

> FRANK: *Run rarebit run.*
> DENIS: *Cheese my lovely.*

The *My Music* follower who thought of this question was Don Smith, a *Radio Times* photographer. Having developed the idea and enlarged on it, he himself came up with *Cheese funny that way*, Handel's *Gruyère you walk* (a bit far-fetched, Don!), *The Brie and I* (that's better) and *The Edam-busters march*. After the broadcast a listener writing from Parkstone, Dorset (Jack Durram) submitted the ingenious Noel Coward song *Nina fromage-entina*!

Turning our attention to the legal profession, how about a signature tune for a judge, a QC, a lawyer: any of those people who not only uphold the law but also make a comfortable living out of it?

> A Hampstead listener put forward this idea, and started the ball rolling with *Guilty*, *Putting on the writs*, Bing Crosby's *Pleas*, and *Won't you come home, Old Bailey?* The winning suggestion, in my view, was the injunction to the legal profession itself: *Bar – bar black sheep*.

Can you think of an appropriate signature tune for a woodman: a member of the Forestry Commission?

> I suspect this idea might have been born out of the old Pat and Mike joke: 'It says here *Tree fellers wanted*. What a pity there's only the two of us!' Anyway, the viewer who put up the idea suggested *Oak-lahoma*, or anything by

Bark. Denis had an enchanting suggestion for a song to be sung by a squirrel: *I was born in a trunk.*

Finally for this chapter (or indeed any other chapter, in a sense), a signature tune for the National Union of Undertakers and Funeral Directors.

> JOHN: *After you've gone.*
> IAN: *Oh what a beautiful morning.*
> DENIS: *I'm walking behind you.*

To which after some thought I could only add a song of the 1920s called *I don't care what you used to be, I know what you are today.* Then Denis came back with the ultimate choice of theme tune for an undertaker: *Catch you now, dig you later.*

I should add that one or two correspondents thought the subject an unsuitable one for levity. I had respect for their view, even for the one who complained that making puns on such a topic was 'a grave error'. That's the trouble with puns: they creep up on you when you're not looking.

What Me? — Sing?

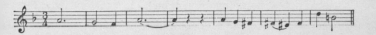

David Franklin having named his autobiography after the official description of his voice – *Basso Cantante* – Denis summarized his own voice as being that of a *Basso can't-hardly*. Frank observed quite early in our first series that 'Denis singing sounds like a moorhen with its leg caught', and went on to call himself 'a light mezzo-baritone with vegetable connections'.

'Do I get a mark for neatness?' inquired Denis humbly, after his first-ever attempt at a song in Programme 1. Not neatness, perhaps, but certainly courage . . . And charm, too, as the many listeners and viewers who have demanded a 'Denis Norden Sings' LP will testify.

By tradition, each edition of *My Music* ends with singing. Frank and Denis oblige with some old favourite from music-hall or Tin Pan Alley; John and Ian offer a verse or a stanza of something more solid from their respective tenor or bass-baritone repertoires.

The question I am most often asked is whether these final songs are rehearsed. The answer is no, they are not rehearsed. (If they were, they would be better!) On the other hand, they are not exactly unplanned. It would be unthinkable that a reasonably entertaining and professional show such as ours should end with the following exchange:

> STEVE: Ian, will you sing for us Toselli's *Serenata*?
> IAN: No. I can't remember it.
> STEVE: Well, that brings us to the end of another edition of *My Music* . . .

No, such an anti-climax really is unthinkable. In order to

ensure that nothing of the sort happens, I keep a running list of
songs which I know the contestants can remember, or have at
least heard of. I then fire at them my choice of song for that
particular week, secure in the knowledge that they can make a
passable stab at the thing, or in John and Ian's case, more than
passable.

Planned, then, but not rehearsed. And that is why we call
those final songs the Party Pieces: somehow it seems the appropriate expression.

Talking of singing, David Franklin once demonstrated an
interesting vocal exercise involving the tune of the National
Anthem, especially useful as a test of a singer's ability to hold
his pitch through a succession of mental key-changes. What you
do, David explained, is to sing *God save the Queen* – to la-la words
if you like – but beginning each new phrase *on the note with which
the previous phrase ended*. Notating the result, you get this:

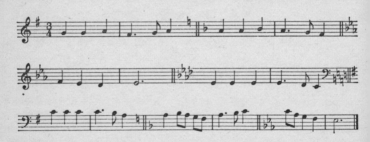

A good test of sight-singing, as well as of pitch-holding.

Before leaving the subject of sight-singing, let me quote a
letter from Hugh Shirreff, of Wincanton, Somerset, whose
mother was a gifted musician. Principally a pianist, she nevertheless went for an audition to sing with the Croydon Choral
Society and was interviewed by the composer Samuel Coleridge-
Taylor. After the audition he offered her a curious back-handed
compliment which, not unnaturally in the circumstances, she
never forgot. 'If everyone read like you,' said the composer, 'I
wouldn't mind if everyone sang like you!'

Maybe Denis should learn to read music.

While we are on the subject of singing, what is oratorio?

DENIS: It comes from the Latin, Steve. *Ora* means 'orror. *Torio* is a bull. So Oratorio is 'orror-bull.

What is a yodel and how did it originate?

A rapid change from falsetto to chest-note, which originated, I have always imagined, when a Swiss mountain guide sat on a crampon. To this piece of information Frank added that a good way to practise yodelling is to ride a bike with a flat tyre and no saddle.

Ian, have you ever had occasion to use the services of a souffleur?

IAN: Yes indeed, as prompter in a French or German opera house, or in an Italian theatre where they call him a *maestro suggeritore*. Opera singers sometimes complain about prompters, particularly the ones they call 'fair-weather prompters', who are fine as long as everything is going well and none of the principals has lost his place, but not so good in a crisis. There was once a lady prompter – or should it be promptress? who was engaged by a certain opera house on the Continent. The first time the soloists lost their place in a complicated scene, she held her hands to her forehead and exclaimed dramatically 'Wrong! Wrong!'

What is a shake?

A shake is the noise a jelly would make if a jelly could make a noise, Frank suggested.

The musical historian Doctor Burney reported that a badly-done shake is known in Italy as a *tosse di capra*, meaning a goat's cough!

───────

What is a roulade?

A rapid vocal run sung to a single syllable. The essayist Addison, having suffered as a listener from a great number of roulades, wrote ' I have known the word "and" pursued through the whole gamut; have been entertained with many a melodious "the", "for" and "from", to the eternal honour of our English particles.'

───────

What is a coup de glotte?

David was at home in this one. A *coup de glotte*, he explained, is a device used by singers. The performer builds up a supply of air in the windpipe, and then opens it in order to make a tremendous attack on a vowel. Literally, it is a blow on the glottis. ' I did it once too often,' he said, 'and had to go to hospital with a broken leg.'

───────

What is a counter tenor?

A counter tenor, according to Denis, is anybody who can count to ten. A more correct (though less entertaining) answer is that the counter tenor is a relatively rare male voice, higher than a normal tenor, popular in England in Handel's time and revived in this century. Some people say that it differs from the male alto voice in employing not *falsetto* but an extension of the normally produced voice.

Which Nightingale died at Malvern in 1887?

The Swedish Nightingale, as she was known: Jenny Lind (Mrs Otto Goldschmidt). She is commemorated by a plaque in Westminster Abbey which was placed between those of Shakespeare and Byron – not a bad place to be.

Apart from the fact that they were both singers, what did Chaliapin and Dame Clara Butt have in common?

FRANK: They both came from Australia except Chaliapin. Furthermore they both came from Russia except Clara Butt. If there is yet a further connection, could it be that they were both born on the same day?

It could. The day was 1 February 1873. It has to be added, though, that Dame Clara was not born in Australia but at Southwick, near Brighton. Frank was thinking of Nellie Melba.

Which musical instrument involves the use of a length of Eustachian tube?

DENIS: You think I don't know what a Eustachian tube is, don't you?

STEVE: That's what I think.

DENIS: It's the tube at Euston stachian.

But he did know that the musical instrument concerned was the human voice. The Eustachian tube lies between the pharynx and the ear. Named after an anatomist called Eustachio, I read that 'it is partly osseous but chiefly cartilaginous'. One hardly knows whether to be glad or sorry.

What can you tell me about The Two Grenadiers?

> FRANK: One doesn't want to encourage rumours, but I agree that there has been some talk. For that matter there's been some talk of Alexander and some of Hercules. Of Hector and Lysander, and such great names as these. But of all the . . .

> Here I brought the meeting to order, and explained that Schumann set to music the poem by Heine. It concerns two grenadiers making their way to France after imprisonment in Russia.

Where will I find the Trout?

> At the end of a Highland reel, of course, said Denis. Also in a book of Schubert songs. (Yes, and in one of his quintets, too.)

What begins with the injunction 'Come ye daughters . . .'?

> J. S. Bach's *St Matthew Passion*. One of our regular supporters in Ely sent me a newspaper review in which the critic had been complaining about the translation of Bach's masterpiece into English from its original German. The headline read 'Difficulty of Passion in English.'

David, where was I sitting one day, weary and ill at ease, and what were my fingers doing?

> DAVID: Heaven give me self-discipline. [But he got it

right, of course: I was referring to Sullivan's *The Lost Chord*.]

———

Who wrote, 'I am jumping about my room for joy! If it turns out to be half as good as I believe it to be, how pleased I shall be!'?

FRANK: It's from the Preface to *Genesis*.

When I could restore order and the audience was fairly quiet again, I explained, for the record, that the lines were written by Mendelssohn in a letter to Jenny Lind, after he had completed Part 1 of his *Elijah*. But Frank's answer remains one of even his most splendid inspirations.

When the *My Music* team was invited to take part in the centenary celebrations commemorating the birth of Miss Lilian Baylis, we recorded a special programme from the stage of Sadler's Wells Theatre. It was a big night for all of us, and a BBC executive, George Steedman, created for the occasion a special invitation ticket.

In Celebration of the Centenary of the Birth of Miss Lilian Baylis

The Governors of the Sadler's Wells Foundation
desire the pleasure of your company
on Saturday, the 27th of April, 1974,
at a quarter past 8 in the evening
in Sadler's Wells Theatre

on which occasion

A QUIZZICAL ENTERTAINMENT FOR WIRELESS BROADCASTING

entitled

MY MUSIC

will be given by

Mr. Frank MUIR	Mr. Denis NORDEN
Mr. Ian WALLACE	Mr. John AMIS

Mr. Steve RACE being in the Chair;

the whole got up under the Direction of

Mr. Tony SHRYANE

and under the August Patronage of the Fourth Network
and the Transcription Services of the

British Broadcasting Corporation

for the Diversion of a distinguished Audience,
and will at the same time be RECORDED upon the
new Magnetical, Mobile, Multiple,
TAPE MACHINE
(operated by the Transcription Recording Unit)
for the later Edification of the Listening Classes
(who may hear it upon the aether at five minutes past 11
on Friday morning, the 10th of May).

There follows an Interval for Refreshment,
after which will be performed

A Surprise Entertainment

by a Performer of Quality.

*The doors of the Theatre and the Refreshment Rooms will be
opened to the Public at half past 6, when a light collation and
alcoholic beverages are to be had.*

Carriages at a quarter past 11	Admit bearer	STALLS Seat No

The thought of being asked to sing on the opera-impregnated boards at Sadler's Wells was almost too much for Denis Norden, but we got him on stage in the end and I know he enjoyed the evening, especially the 'Surprise Entertainment by a Performer of Quality', which turned out to be by our own Ian Wallace. Ian gave a compressed version of his splendid 'Evening with' entertainment, his personal accompanist David Money assisting at the piano.

For me, apart from the thrill of being on the stage at such an historic opera house, it was a golden opportunity to indulge my taste for history and study the long and strange story of Mr Sadler, his wells, and the various entertainments that had taken place on the site. Dennis Arundell's *The Story of Sadler's Wells* was an enormous help to me in setting the questions. For example, I learnt about Hiram Fisteman.

Towards the end of the eighteenth century in the theatre which stood on the site of Sadler's Wells Theatre, the manager used on certain occasions to go to the back of the stalls and shout: 'Is Hiram Fisteman here? Is Hiram Fisteman here?' Question: who was Hiram Fisteman?

The answer is that there was no such person. He didn't exist. The manager's words were a code signal to the actors on stage that they should immediately bring the performance to a close. It meant that there were enough people waiting outside the theatre to make a second house.

I also discovered that in 1710 it was possible to get into the theatre for sixpence. And how much was the cheapest seat in Lilian Baylis's day? – I know from personal experience as a student: still sixpence.

During our recording we naturally talked a good deal about ballet as well as about opera. The conversation turned to some of the more avant-garde dance groups which now visit London, and indeed have invaded that very stage from time to time. Denis was reminded of the remark made by Sir Robert Helpmann on the tiresome subject of nude ballet dancers: 'In the nature of things, not everything stops when the music does.'

The Piano Medleys

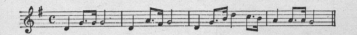

JOHN: How long do they take you to work out, Steve?

STEVE: Oh, it's hard to say. One tune seems to lead naturally to another. I sometimes think of them in the bath, or
when riding on top of a bus . . .

DENIS: How do you get the piano up those twisted stairs?

My piano medleys have become a regular part of the *My Music*
recordings ever since 1972, when the celeste beside my chairman's chair was replaced by a piano. In devising them, I find the
trick is to glide from one tune to another with as little fuss as
possible, finding perhaps a three-note 'pivot' which is common
to both melody lines, or even just a chord which links them in
some significant way. People have been very kind about the
medleys over the years, and one princess (who shall be nameless)
inquired how I thought them up. The answer was that they just
'come' . . . (Ma'am).

Here are the melody lines of two typical piano medleys, which
the reader might like to hum or play his way through. The titles
are listed afterwards for checking (or cheating) purposes.

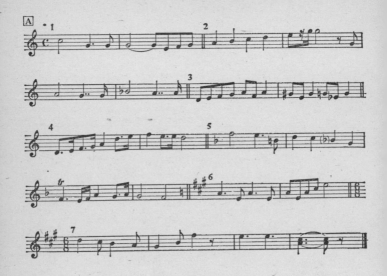

Piano Medley A

1. *Prelude: The Mastersingers* (Wagner)
2. *The Lord High Executioner* (Sullivan)
3. *In the hall of the mountain king* (Grieg)
4. *Charlie is my darling* (Trad.)
5. *Wedding march* (Mendelssohn)
6. *Eine kleine Nachtmusik* (Mozart)
7. *Boney was a warrior* (Trad.)

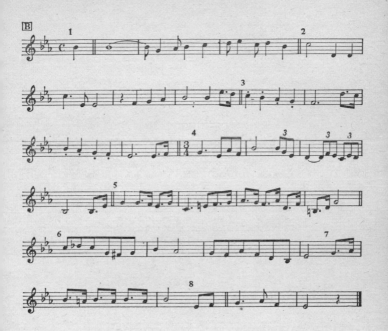

Piano Medley B

1. *La paloma* (Yradier)
2. *None but the weary heart* (Tchaikovsky)
3. *Caro nome – Rigoletto* (Verdi)
4. *Una voce poco fa – The Barber of Seville* (Rossini)
5. *5th Symphony, 2nd movement* (Beethoven)
6. *I don't want to play in your yard* (Petrie)
7. *Minuet in G* (Beethoven)
8. *The star-spangled banner* (attrib. various)

Composers: The Truth at Last

When I told Frank that it was André Previn who composed the song *Goodbye, Charlie* he replied, 'Well, nobody's perfect.' So much for composers . . . of whom the following has been said in one or another of our programmes.

The French composer Jacques Ibert was awarded the Légion d'honneur for something that is considered rather rare among musicians. What was it?

DENIS: He could play the double bass from the inside.
Conceivably so. At any rate it is a nice thought. But actually M. Ibert got his award for courage in the First World War.

———

Can you distinguish between two Schuberts and a Schubart?

John certainly could. Franz Peter Schubert, the great songwriter and symphonist; Franz (or François) Schubert, the nineteenth-century violinist and composer of a piece called *The Bee*; and C. F. D. Schubart, eighteenth-century court musical director. Mention of the Schuberts/ Schubart reminded John of something that happened to the great Emil Gilels after he had given a piano recital. Someone came up to him and said, 'Mr Gilels, you're a knowledgeable musician. Can you answer me a musical question? It's something I've always wanted to know: should the composer's name be pronounced Schu-*bert* or Schu-*mann*?'

Which great composer, who incidentally gave his name to a steak, wrote practically nothing for the last forty years of his life? And how was it that he died at the age of nineteen?

Frank suggested that he was a Hamburger. But the steak innovator turned out to be Rossini, who was born on Leap Day 1792, and so (like W. S. Gilbert's Frederic) enjoyed fewer birthdays than the rest of us. On reflection Frank decided that Rossini had a steak named after him because of one of his compositions: *Minute Waltz*. ('Well done!' cried a member of the audience.)

What happened when Vaughan Williams decided that he needed, in his own words, 'a little French polish'?

It was in 1908. He went to Paris, though already quite well known himself, to seek some practical composing advice from Maurice Ravel. It is reported that as they parted, not having got on particularly well, Ravel said to V.W. somewhat condescendingly, 'Now will you write me a little minuet in the Mozart style for when we next meet?' And Vaughan Williams replied 'No.'

Which of Puccini's operas was composed posthumously?

> IAN: None of them. I'm told it is very difficult to compose after one has died.
>
> FRANK: Mind you, it is possible to de-compose.

Which great composer died in Great Portland Street, near Broadcasting House, London?

> Weber. In the ensuing discussion Denis observed that Carl Maria von Weber was called 'Carl Maria' because his father wanted a boy but his mother wanted a girl, so they compromised.

Which famous composer married twice and was the father of twenty children?

> DENIS: Sounds more like a producer than a composer.
>
> David reminded us of the immortal schoolboy howler about Bach: 'He had twenty children and in between he used to practise on a spinster in the attic.'

Which composer was born in Northampton in 1901?

> Edmund Rubbra (as opposed to William Alwyn, who was born there in 1905, and Malcolm Arnold in 1921).
>
> Rubbra once confessed to a reporter that as a young student he wrote a piece of music with a title which he later came to regret. It was called *Nature's call*.
>
> Finding myself sitting next to Rubbra at a concert, I mentioned the piece. 'That's not the worst,' he told me.

'Another early work of mine was a choral piece called *When last I went*. I regret that one even more!'

———

Why was Vivaldi called the Red Priest?

FRANK: He really was a priest, was he?
STEVE: Yes.
FRANK: Well, they called him the Red Priest because he used to blush rather readily at Confession.

(I read with some pleasure on a record sleeve that 'for thirty-six years Vivaldi was employed at a music school for girls in Venice, and this gave him wonderful opportunities for experimenting'!)

———

He composed eighteen string quartets, of which numbers 14 and 15 can be performed simultaneously, thereby creating a string octet. Who was he?

He was Darius Milhaud, and John identified him immediately. Ian then recalled appearing in a London Opera Club production of Milhaud's *Le Pauvre Matelot*. 'As an old sailor,' said Ian, 'I had been given at one point a bit of very deliberate stage business. I had to walk slowly across the stage, pick up a chair, take it to the wall, walk back, pick up a lamp from the table, go back to the wall, climb on to the chair and hang the lamp on a nail. All the time Jennifer Vyvyan was singing away centre-stage.

'On the first night I duly entered, took the chair to the wall, went back to the table, picked up the lamp, took it to the wall, stepped on the chair, raised the lamp slowly above my head . . . and only then did I find that there was no nail.

'So there was nothing for it but to walk back with my lamp to the table and put it back where I'd got it from. All the time I could hear voices from the audience asking one another "What's he doing? What's he *doing*?"'

———

In one of the London city churches there is a stained glass window in commemoration of a composer. One of the scenes illustrated in the window shows a herd of Australian cows. What is all that about?

Presumably, thought Denis, whoever-it-was composed a piece for Australian cows, or Horn Concerto. (To which Frank added that perhaps it was the song inspired by the cow that swallowed a bottle of ink, *Mooed indigo*.)

The composer's name was John Ireland. The memorial window to his memory is in the Musicians' Chapel of the Church of the Holy Sepulchre and depicts various compositions of his – a seascape representing *Sea Fever*, for instance. The cows commemorate his film score for *The Overlanders*.

———

Can you think of a composer's name which is palindromic?

Not only our contestants but also a listener or two joined in the search for a composer's name which reads the same forwards as backwards. We ended up with Joaquin *Nin*, Max *Reger* (some people thought palindromism was the best thing about him), Frank *Lessel*, a banjoist called Harry *Reser*, an obscure composer named *Reyer*, and the American Seymour *Barab*. So far as I know there is no composer named *Kok*, and a musically-inclined relative of the *Koekkoek* family of painters would not quite qualify as a palindrome, useful though he might be in multiple-set Scrabble.

———

Tell me something about Meyerbeer.

And John dutifully did. When Meyerbeer died, his nephew went to see Rossini with a Funeral March and asked the great man to give his opinion of it. After looking at the score with lacklustre eyes, Rossini said, 'Well, it's very pleasant, my boy, very pleasant. But don't you think it would have been better if *you* had died and your uncle had composed the Funeral March?'

What did Richter do on the staircase for Liszt's daughter?

A question like this brightens the proceedings now and again, I feel. What Richter did was to play the trumpet part in the *Siegfried Idyll* on the morning of Christmas Day 1870, as Cosima Wagner (née Liszt) lay in bed with her infant son. Wagner and his group of friends played it on the stairs outside her bedroom.

Frank was wrong about this story. He thought that Richter on the staircase had said to Cosima, 'Let's make a little Liszt.'

We all know the opera called Tannhäuser *by Wagner, but that's not its full title.* Tannhäuser and . . . *What?*

DENIS: And the Forty Thieves?
FRANK: And Son?
The Truth: And the Contest of Song at the Wartburg.

---

*Born in Ireland, he is best known as the composer of Maritana. He
was a great traveller. In Sydney he received a fee of 200 sheep for
a concert. In Chile he rode 125 miles in eleven hours, with thirteen
changes of horse, to keep an engagement to perform. In the end he
courted an Irish nun . . . and then married her sister. Who was he?*

> IAN: We're a very large family, and the great thing about
> my family is that none of us is related to one another. This
> particular Wallace was related only to himself: William.
> (William Vincent Wallace, 1812–56.)

Did Smetana have a successful evening on 30 May 1866?

> DENIS: Indeed he did. One thing about Smetana; he
> certainly knew which side his Bride was Bartered.

Denis was lucky: the pun gave the right answer.
Smetana's big night in Prague was a huge success, and
one hopes the following morning's newspapers spelt his
name correctly. When the poor man visited England he is
said to have been driven mad by people who would put
the stress on the second syllable of his surname instead of
on the first. Smet-*Ar*-na they called him. 'No, no,' he
would remonstrate, '*Smet*-ana, please, *Smet*-ana.' But it
was to no avail, until in the end he started singing to them
the finale theme from Beethoven's 8th Symphony:

So Much for Jazz

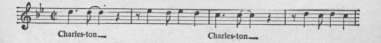

Charles-ton___   Charles-ton___

No member of the *My Music* panel knows much about jazz, so for all their chairman's affection for it, that type of music has not featured much in the programmes. It is depressing to ask a question about Bix Beiderbecke and be asked, 'What was the first name again?' Even Denis, who is about the nearest we can boast to a jazz buff, only seems to know the names of the band-leaders. As for the jazz repertoire, he is every bit as hazy as on certain types of music at the other end of the social scale. 'If you can't foxtrot to it, I don't know it,' he says. The only exceptions are jazz evergreens which happen also to be Tin Pan Alley hits like (to quote Denis again) the one that begins 'Zhivago, Zhivago, that toddlin' town . . .'

On the other hand no member of my teams has ever been inhibited by mere ignorance. Read on.

How does a drummer make a sizzle?

> FRANK: He spits on a hot clarinet. Alternatively he cuts small holes in a cymbal and hangs nuts and bolts from it, together with one or two paperclips, to make it go Szzzz...

———

What is a hi-hat?

> Like the poetry of Mallarmé, said Denis (with the easy confidence of the *My Word* panellist), it's one symbol on

top of another. And a drummer uses it to make his *Oom-cha*.

Dead right. (Though I wouldn't know about Mallarmé.) A hi-hat consists of two cymbals, one above the other, operated by a foot pedal and placed on the left of the drummer's kit, rather than on the right, where a lay person might reasonably expect to find it.

Which clarinet-playing bandleader married both Ava Gardner and Lana Turner (though at different times)?

Artie Shaw. A correspondent recalled serving under an army sergeant who was nicknamed Artie Shaw, because when calling his men to attention he used to shout at them: 'Squad – Artie – Shaw!'

Another most welcome story arose from that and was sent in by Colin Sewell of Mitcham, Surrey. Mr Sewell had served in the Royal Navy in the First World War. The commanding officer of his ship was, he said, 'a swine of the first order'.

Some years after the war ended he met a bandsman of his acquaintance, who told Mr Sewell he was on his way to play at the Captain's funeral.

'What are you going to play? – *Happy days are here again*?'

'No,' replied the bandsman. '*Blaze away*!'

Frank, what is a jug band?

FRANK: It's the house band at one of Her Majesty's Prisons.

In the absence of a bass or tuba player, some jazz groups in the 1920s used a jug, which emitted a hollow bass-like sound when one blew across the neck. The Muppets occasionally use one still.

———

Can you name one of the record hits of Nellie Lutcher?

Hurry on down or *A fine brown frame* would do nicely. A radio listener in Willesden, London, wrote to me to say that when the latter tune was popular she went into a record store to buy a copy, and asked the assistant, 'Have you got *A fine brown frame?*'

To which he replied: 'No, lady, just a small white skinny one.'

———

What have (or had) they in common? – Jack Dupree, Jack Doyle and Joe Frazier?

Quite a far cry from jazz, I grant you, but at least Champion Jack Dupree sang a mean blues. They were all singing boxers.

Denis recalled that Jack Doyle had a double career as pugilist and Irish tenor. In fact a cruel boxing correspondent once observed that instead of singing *Mother Machree*, Jack Doyle would have done better to have fought her.

———

What is a plunger?

A kind of brass mute used in jazz and swing bands. This brought a scholarly footnote from Frank, who pointed out that in the eighteenth century the orchestral musicians could only afford one mute between them, so they used to club together to buy one, and kept it between their chairs in a bucket of disinfectant.

You can read all about it, said Frank, in Gray's *Elegy*, at the words: 'Some mute, in glorious Milton . . .'

———

What is the theme music used by the Harlem Globetrotters?

Ignoring Frank's splendidly unlikely suggestion (*Only a rose*) Denis and I agreed that it was *Sweet Georgia Brown*, performed on a record by a group called Bones and his Brothers.

This led to a discussion on signature tunes in general, and on who could claim to have first thought of the idea. Most people believe that the first signature tune was *Lustige Bruder* (*Jolly brothers*), which the great Albert Whelan used to whistle as he came on stage, while slowly removing his gloves. But Max Beerbohm claimed that the first performer of recent times to have a signature tune was R. G. Knowles, billed as 'the very peculiar American comedian'. Knowles always came on stage in the 1880s and 90s to the music of Mendelssohn's *Wedding march*.

It is typical of the *My Music* 'family feeling' that no sooner had this seemingly forgotten gentleman been mentioned on the air, than I had a letter from his nephew. Yes: Mr Knowles came to London in 1891, appeared at the old Tivoli Theatre, and died in 1918.

———

One of the many show tunes that jazz musicians delight to improvise on is I know that you know. *Who composed it?*

Vincent Youmans. When I pointed out to Denis that the whole sense of the song's title could be changed merely by

re-punctuating it – 'I *know* that, you know' – he came
back with two gems of re-punctuation, or at any rate re-
stress: 'I saw you last night and got that *old* feeling'; and
'Love is *where*? – *You* find it!'

And that reminded both of us of the song that didn't
quite come from *My Fair Lady*: 'We *could* have *danced*
all night!' There is also Shirley Basscy's pained inquiry,
'What, *now*, my love?'

Almost thirty *My Music* addicts wrote to add to the list
a song by Cole Porter, but by then the broadcast was over.
The song? – 'What is this thing *called*, love?'

A Few Technicalities
(and foreign, to boot)

Xenophobia has no place in our ranks, even if we could spell it, and I am proud of my panellists, who welcome questions about foreign musicians almost as readily as if the poor devils were British. So far from patronizing foreigners, we regard them with genuine sympathy, as when Frank Muir was overcome with a sudden feeling of sadness on reflecting that Vincent Van Gogh could never hear Stereo.

Many of the most frequently used technical terms in music were invented by people who did not speak English and therefore had to make do with their own inferior tongues. The resulting expressions are explained in this chapter, especially by Frank and Denis, who, as participants in the *My Word* series, are expert at words and their derivations.

What does con brio *mean?*

FRANK: With cheese.

———

What are piatti?

Ah, said Denis, Italian – yes? In Italian they put an I where other languages would tend to put an L, so *piatti* would really read *platti* – plates. I've got it now. *Piatti* refers to the musical plates. They put cannelloni on one, ravioli on another and lasagna on a third, which gives a different pitch for each dish. Then when they're carrying them into the restaurant people say 'Look darling, they're serving our song.'

———

What is ponticello?

Sul ponticello, or *sul pont*, is an injunction met with in string music, indicating that the performer is to play with his bow close to the bridge.

'A beautiful word,' exclaimed Frank, 'and clearly Italian. *Cello* means little. If a Roman has guests for the evening and they're starting to look bored, he might turn to them after dinner and say "Ponticello? – A little Bridge?"'

———

What is schmaltz?

DENIS: Guy Lombardo's Orchestra playing *Little Lady Makebelieve*.

———

A special imaginary question for Ian Wallace. In her will, Ian, your great aunt writes, 'I leave my best colophonium to my dear nephew Ian.' One day the postman arrives carrying a parcel containing the long-awaited colophonium. On the label it says 'Colophonium for Ian. This side up.' Having opened it, what do you do with it?

Ask silly questions and you get silly answers. Ian knew the answer: you rub it on your fiddle bow. *Colophonium* is the Latin word for rosin.

———

*A different kind of technicality. How many ballet positions are
there?*

> FRANK: Well there's quarter to three and there's three
> o'clock. Then there's ten to two, after which it goes into
> the third dimension.
> STEVE: The nastiest one is twenty-five to five, I should
> think.
> FRANK: There aren't very many, are there? Say six?
> STEVE: Actually five.
> FRANK: Ah but I was speaking of before the war.

What is an entrechat?

> According to David Franklin, an *entrechat* is 'when a chap
> rises in the air and twiddles his feet like an egg-beater. If
> he's still twiddling by the time he hits the ground again,
> he's in dead trouble.'

Denis, what can you tell me about the expression entrechat-dix?

> DENIS: It originated in a production of *Dick Whittington
> and his Cat* at the Paris Opera, when they were auditioning
> for someone to play the cat. Nine cat imitators they tried
> out, without success, until finally the producer, almost in
> despair, called out to the wings 'Entre chat dix . . .'
>   Balletically minded friends tell me that an entrechat-dix
> is a jump from, and ending in, the fifth position, during
> which the feet are crossed ten times before coming to
> earth. Nijinsky was one of the relatively few dancers who
> could do it. Ernie Wise can't, at least not since the
> operation.

Frank, what is a bébé?

FRANK: It's what transforms a hubbé into a daddé.
Also the French name for a small upright piano, but that's much less fun.

———

How would you play a quijada de burro?

I would play it rhythmically and while wearing a frilly shirt, said Denis, immediately latching on to the right idea. Then he added 'But because of that word *burro* I'd be careful to play it from the rear. Right?'
Right enough. A *quijada de burro* is the jawbone of an ass: a Cuban percussion instrument.

———

What does a capella *mean?*

DENIS: It means to do it without anybody accompanying you, which is always a very big moment in any little boy's life. In a musical connection I suppose it means to sing unaccompanied. [Literally 'in the style of church music'.]

———

What does the expression pièces de sauvetage *come from?*

From the opera world of Napoleonic times, meaning operas with last-minute rescues, as in *Fidelio*. Literally 'rescue-pieces'.

Frank, where does that expression come from?
FRANK: From France.

———

What do you do, Denis, when it says volti subito?

I switch off at the mains as quickly as I can. [Ian would turn the page of the music quickly.]

———

What is a verbunko?

IAN: You've come to the right person, Steve. I had one once on my foot. I picked it up at the swimming bath, they're very nasty and it won't get better if you pick it.

But the answer I know you're after, Steve, is different. *Verbunko* is what they say when the German radio station, which is known as the Telefunken, breaks down. 'Der Telefunken,' they announce, 'is verbunko.'

I had not the heart to tell Ian that the verbunko is a Hungarian dance done by hussars in uniform in order to stimulate recruiting. It is one of those answers that no one wants to hear.

———

If, as a performer, you were asked to take off your sourdine, *what would you do?*

DENIS: I would fight it all the way, because you can get on in show business without going in for that sort of thing. (The truth: he would remove his mute.)

———

What is the difference between a tscheng *and a* tschung?

A *tscheng* is a Chinese mouth-organ, but a *tschung* is a Chinese gong. And just to confuse things, a *chang* is a Persian harp. For Frank, though, a *tscheng* is the sound made by dropping barbecued spare-rib bones on to a Cantonese cymbal, while a *tschung* is pronounced *choon* and is a melody played by Chinese musicians on a comb and rice-paper.

———

Finally, what and whence is a bergamasque?

It is a rustic dance, as mentioned by Bottom in *A Midsummer Night's Dream*, in imitation of the peasants of Bergamo, home of the Commedia dell'Arte.

But not to Denis. For him – and forever afterwards for me too – a berga-masque is what you put over your face when you're eating a Wimpy.

Musical Mysteries Explained

Molto espress.

Lil-lie Lang-try, I love you. . . .

Anyone who listens to our programme for a number of years either goes mad or learns a great deal about music. Not only music, either: I never expected to know that the Icelandic word for a journalist is a *blether-mesiter*, but I know it now, thanks to an aside from Frank Muir. On a strictly musical level I have learnt from a viewer in Englefield Green, Surrey, that a useful tip for following music in five-four time is to repeat to yourself:

> 'Rim – sky – Kor – sa – kov
> Rim – sky – Kor – sa – kov . . .'

And from Frank I have learnt that a *minor second* is 'the speed at which the National Coal Board can close pits'.

On with the show:

Where would you find an F-hole?

This, according to a happy inspiration on Ian's part, concerns an orchestral instrument known as the hole. The instrument comes in different pitch-sizes: there is an F-hole and a B-flat-hole, for instance.

DENIS: You can buy them holesale, too.

IAN: Now and then you have to sit and listen to a hole concerto.

For the benefit of readers who want the holy correct answer, you would find an F-hole on the belly of a violin

or other string instrument. It allows the vibrating air inside
to escape, thus improving the resonance.

———

What is a harp stop?

Part of the action of a harpsichord, damping the strings
and making the instrument sound rather like a harp,
hence the name. For Frank the answer is simpler, though.
For him, a harp stop is a pair of wirecutters.

———

Where would you find sympathetic strings?

DENIS: As we all know, there is a lot of industrial unrest
around in our symphony orchestras these days. When the
brass players come out on strike you'll sometimes see the
violin section outside the manager's office playing *We shall
overcome*. They're sympathetic strings.

Right, Denis. You would also find them on, say, a sitar,
which has 'extra' strings designed to resonate in sympathy
with those already plucked.

———

What does a barrel organ player do with his left hand?

According to Frank it depends on what the monkey's
doing with his right. On the other hand, it depends a bit
on the strength of his arm. After grinding away for a while
with his right hand on the winding handle, he'll probably
change to his left.

———

What is a postlude?

DENIS: I think I can work my way towards this one. Robert Benchley once wrote a book that had a postface instead of a preface, so I should think it comes at the end rather than at the beginning; a prelude, you might say, that has gone round the back. An example of a postlude would be that bit at the end of *Boiled beef and carrots* that goes 'Diddle-iddle om-pom, diddle-iddle om-pom, How's your father? – All right!'

What is a Scotch snap?

It's a brandy snap made with whisky. Or perhaps you should take a Scotch snap with a McCamera.

No prize is offered for guessing who said that. As he probably didn't know, a Scotch snap is a group of two notes, of which the first is shorter than the second. It is a pattern often met with in Scottish folk music, and it looks like this:

What is immediately above the G string?

Surely the *belly* of the instrument, suggested Frank. [But above, in the pitch sense, you would find the D string, on a violin, viola or cello. On a guitar it would be the B string.]

What is treble-stopping?

> FRANK: It's a frightful morning at the dentist's. Or if you mean in fiddle playing, it involves playing on three strings at (or very nearly at) the same time. It usually sounds rather unpleasant.

Where might you find a saddle?

> This had something to do with Bach, Ian claimed, because he remembered hearing on the radio that there were some 'empty saddles in the old Chorale'. Later Ian homed in on the right answer: you would find a saddle on a violin. It is the ebony bar over which the tail-gut passes.

What is a sitar?

> An Indian string instrument provided with gourds to amplify the sound.
> FRANK: I don't know what a sitar is, but a small one – that's a baby sitar – is someone you get in for the evening when you and your wife want to go to the pictures.

A triplet is three notes played in the time of two or four. What is the word for nine notes in the time of eight?

> John Amis hopefully suggested 'a nono-nanette'. The word is nonuplet.

What is a nonet?

DENIS: A non-et sounds like the unexpired portion of your day's ration.

Actually a nonet is an ensemble of nine performers, or a composition written for them.

———

If the soft pedal halves a piano's volume, what does the loud pedal do?

DENIS: I know what you want me to say but I'm not going to say it. Actually it dips the headlights.

Denis's answer was no more incorrect than most people's. The loud pedal is incorrectly named, and ought rather to be called the sustaining pedal. It sustains the notes played when it is depressed: certainly it does not make them any louder. 'Loud pedal' is probably the most commonly used musical error after *crescendo*, which means not *loud* but *becoming louder*. 'The opposition cheers reached a crescendo' is a nonsense line repeated almost weekly by political journalists.

———

What is a heckelphone?

A bass oboe made initially by the German firm of Heckel. It sounds an octave lower in pitch than the oboe and is rarely met with, though Richard Strauss and Delius called for its use.

All this sailed straight over Denis's head. For him a heckelphone is a loudspeaker used by opponents at a political meeting.

———

MY MUSIC

All right then, can you give me an example of an idiophone?

> DENIS: As it happens, Steve, I can. I would call an idio-
> phone the work of the man who designed telephone boxes
> in such a way that whichever way you approach them the
> door is always on the other side.
>
> Under the official classification of musical instruments
> into groups, an idiophone is struck, shaken or rubbed, as
> in a triangle, cymbal or washboard; drums are mem-
> branophones, violins are chordophones, and wind-blown
> instruments (Aeolian harps, I suppose) are aerophones.

What is a tam-tam?

> A gong. Though according to Frank, *tam-tam* is the sound
> you get when you play the tom-tom on somebody's tum-
> tum.

What does a guitarist do with his left thumb, Frank?

> Keeps it always clean and hygienic, Steve. Just occasion-
> ally he thumps it against the woodwork, as in Spanish
> music. Otherwise I have a feeling that he does nothing
> with his left thumb, other than use it to prevent his
> instrument falling to the ground.

What is a fipple? (Apart from being the mouthpiece of a flute.)

> DENIS: The word comes from a well-known saying which
> goes 'You can pool all the fipple some of the time . . .' Or

is it perhaps based on the fip? Fips, of course, are what you eat with chish.

———

What is a short score?

> IAN: All out for 29 and no extras.
> DENIS: A score with the title-page missing.
> STEVE (*boring as ever*): It's a condensed version of a full score, perhaps with more than one instrument- or voice-part to a stave.

———

What is a full score?

> ALL THE CONTESTANTS IN UNISON: Twenty. Next question!

———

What does the sequence of letters C – G – D – A represent?

> The tuning notes of the viola's or cello's strings. Or to Frank, the letters stand for Coventry Great Dane Association.

———

If E is Dimity, and C is Gaudé, why should one be wary of D?

> This question is for connoisseurs of the whodunit, and my teams, being well read, spotted the allusion straight away.

One would be wary of D because it would be Batty Thomas, the bell that killed three people in Dorothy L. Sayer's thriller *The Nine Tailors*. The bells' names, in order, were *Gaudé, Sabaoth, John, Jericho, Jubilee, Dimity, Batty Thomas* and *Tailor Paul*. ('And don't forget *Lust*,' added Denis. 'That's the one everybody puts first.')

What is a tucket?

IAN: It's what you get in exchange for your fare on a Glasgow tram. [Also a flourish or fanfare.]

What do musicians mean when they talk about hairpins?

DENIS: They're quoting a Fred Astaire song called *It only hairpins when I dance with you*. Wait a minute, though – they're crescendo and diminuendo signs, aren't they? And even I know what the signs look like. They look like two crocodiles approaching one another with their mouths open.

What is a relative minor?

IAN: Could it be a pit pony's uncle?
STEVE: In a word, no.
IAN: Then it's the minor equivalent of a major key.
STEVE: In another word, yes.

------

*In a book about medieval percussion instruments I came across a
reference to* nakers. *Hence my question to Frank: how do you play*
nakers?

FRANK: I hope you don't clash them together!

What is a mounted cornet?

DENIS: You're never going to get me to say it's a man on a
horse eating an ice-cream! It's a very large trumpet-type
cornet, which is so large and tubular that you have to sit
astride it in order to play the thing. If you happen to be
wearing thin trousers it can be a nasty shock to the system.

(Oh dear, these necessary explanations!) A mounted
cornet is an organ stop, mounted high on a soundboard of
its own so as to be better heard in cornet voluntaries. No
doubt there is also a less tedious definition concerned with
army bandsmen.

How did the word polytonality *originate?*

Many answers have been offered over the years, but few as
convincing as the Frank Muir suggestion. According to
him, William Byrd, the famous Elizabethan composer,
was accustomed to write music with his favourite parrot
perched on his shoulder. (That was why he was known as
'Byrd'.)

One day the parrot fell off his shoulder on to the key-
board, and at the moment of impact hit one chord with its
left toe and quite another with its right toe. Byrd called
the result Poly – toe – nality.

A famous American, when in Europe, saw some musical glasses being played. Much impressed, he constructed a mechanical version for himself. Who was he, and what did he call his glass-playing device when he got it back to America?

DENIS: He called it 'my collection of broken glass'. I suppose he was the chap who does all the inventions, Pat Pending.

No, it wasn't Pat Pending. (Nor was it the man who owns all the lorries, Max Speed.) It was Benjamin Franklin.

———

What is an Alp-horn?

FRANK: A very long round wooden instrument with a hole through the middle, sometimes having a bend towards the far end to support it. Laughing Swiss peasantry in leather knickers blow down it at dusk to call home the Gruyère cheeses.

All true. And nowadays, I am told, the performers sometimes fool gullible tourists like ourselves by having an accomplice across the valley to provide a spurious echo!

———

Various degrees of the scale have technical names. What do musicians mean when they talk about the supertonic?

FRANK: One that comes with the gin already in it.

Sir, You Err

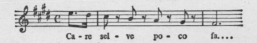

Ca - re sel - ve po - co fa....

'Great men may err wildly, yet not be mad.'
Coleridge

We (or more frequently, I) have erred from time to time in *My
Music*. Some of the questions have been wrong; even more of
the answers. I have uttered staggering untruths with perfect
confidence, denied marks where marks were due, thrown them
around like confetti where they were unmerited, and generally
clotted my bopybook. This chapter lists some of the more
glaring errors, and throws in for good measure a few of the
happier errors and misprints that have been sent in by correspondents over the years.

But first my apologies. My apologies for pronouncing the
Furry Dance at Helston as if it were covered with fur, instead of
making the word rhyme with *hurry*. My apologies for calling
Peter Doody, the 'I gotta motter' jockey in *The Arcadians*, by
the name of Cully, when I should have known that *cully* was
merely an Edwardian word meaning *mate* or *pal*. My apologies
for getting confused over whether John Peel's coat was gay or
grey, and my thanks to all those people who wrote in to correct
me, among them a descendant of the original poet responsible.
Rather more qualified apologies to the listener who complained
that someone sang 'Britannia *rules* the waves' (instead of *rule*)
when we were merely enjoying a complicated singsong, taking a
syllable each and seeing how far we could get. (Some people are
really rather determined fault-finders. And shall I get a letter
pointing out that *fault-finders* ought not to be hyphenated?)

One complaint I utterly reject is that I show special favour to
Ian or Frank, or for that matter to Denis or John: the accusations
are more or less evenly divided across the foursome. What our
correspondents sometimes forget is that John is a musicological

expert in the sense that Ian would never claim to be. Similarly Denis may be termed an expert in Nostalgia music, spending a considerable amount of his professional life in researching it, while Frank is merely an interested listener to music which happens to please him. I try to ask them questions which they can *just* answer, and to help them equally if that answer remains tantalizingly on the tip of the tongue. However, if you think about it, it is easier to find a light clue to help Ian identify *William Tell* than an equally helpful guide for John when he is momentarily struggling to name Grétry's *Céphale et Procris*. Similarly, the single word 'Yip' would be enough to lead Denis to the song *Brother, can you spare a dime?* whereas if I said 'Yip' to Frank he would probably reply 'Gesundheit'.

I had 'a little local difficulty' (in Harold Macmillan's splendidly cool phrase) with Scots listeners over the exact location of Maxwelton Braes in *Annie Laurie*. As a correspondent put it: 'Maxwelton is a house in Dumfriesshire; Macwelltown is in Kirkcudbright.' Just so. I also stood corrected by Geordies as to the precise date of Blaydon Races, as sung – a trifle indistinctly, to tell the truth – by Owen Brannigan.

A great gaping pitfall of error concerns one of Britain's best-loved theatrical composers, Sir Arthur Sullivan, 'the well-known octoroon composer', as a contemporary biography blandly described him. The fact is that Sullivan was not directly responsible for all the Savoy overtures, handing over their construction and orchestration to various assistants and workaday arrangers of the period, even though the resulting overtures used Sullivan's own themes. A Gilbert and Sullivan specialist named James Gillespie was kind enough to send me a check-list of Savoy overture sources, showing that writers other than Sullivan were involved in the overtures to *The Sorcerer*, *HMS Pinafore*, *The Pirates of Penzance*, *Princess Ida*, *The Mikado* and *Ruddigore*.

So to the question 'Who wrote the overture to *The Mikado*?' one might truthfully reply 'Hamilton Clarke'.

Similarly:

Who composed Haydn's Toy Symphony *and Purcell's* Trumpet
Voluntary?

Leopold Mozart and Jeremiah Clarke respectively.

Who composed the famous Albinoni Adagio?

Giazotto, basing it on an original fragment by Albinoni.

Who composed Brahm's Cradle Song?

We don't know, but it wasn't Brahms. He merely
arranged it.

Mistakes in song lyrics and titles, often made by children, have
been among the delights of my chairman's and question-setter's
postbag. Starting within the family, my very own nephew,
Daniel, when a small boy, delighted his father – and his Uncle
Steve – by singing one Christmas '*Half* the herald angels sing',
proving that inflation can affect the heavenly choir just as surely
as choirs on earth. When I reported Danny's version of the
hymn on the air, a listener in Dunstable wrote that he had overheard his granddaughter in a further variation which went
'Hark, the *hairy* angels sing'.

One of our regular listeners in South Africa, Mrs Elizabeth
Randolph, was once asked by her small daughter to sing 'the
song about a lion in bed'. This defeated her, until the next time
she heard on the radio:

> '*Three li'l chillun,*
> *A lion in bed . . .*'

– from *Shortnin' bread.*

A supporter of ours once wrote to say that his mother had a
way of singing songs to herself while doing the chores – as indeed
many people do – but without really listening to what words she
was singing. He remembered hearing her version of Ronald
Gourlay's song *The dickie-bird hop* in which the first line had
somehow become 'Oh the chirruping of the birdies when they're

sick in a tree . . .' Another favourite of hers was the more senti-
mental song that went 'I noticed when you kissed me that both
your feet were wet . . .'

The errors extend to printed as well as to spoken words. A
correspondent wrote to tell me that while glancing at an advertisement for some performances by the English National Opera,
he noticed that the first three days of the week had been listed in
his newspaper as:

> Monday: *Rhinegold*
> Tuesday: *Valkyrie*
> Wednesday: *Ziegfeld*.

Talking of opera, a *My Music* viewer reported that while
passing an opera house in Stockholm he pointed to the poster
outside and asked a Swedish friend what was being performed
there. The friend translated it from the Swedish: it was, he said,
The Amazing Whistle, by Mozart.

Mr R. L. Neesam wrote from Welwyn Garden City to tell us
about a printed programme which advertised a selection from
The Mikano. He also enclosed the photostat programme of a
local band concert which included two gems by Gilbert and
Sullivan: *When the foreman bares his steel* – (those shop stewards
get more powerful by the minute) – and, from *The Gondoliers*,
the much-loved *Garotte*.

From Sussex, Mollie Ashworth quoted a concert programme
which read:

> Overture: *Di Ballo* – Sir A. Sullivan
> Concerto in D – Major Bach

As for me, in more years than I care to remember around the
musical scene, I have come across some enjoyable misprints,
and especially mis-typings. As I told Denis Norden in one of
our programmes, who could fail to go around humming these? –

> *Three cons in the fountain*
> *I'm in the wood for love*
> *I've got you under my ski*
> or
> *You were meat for me*

– the last-mentioned song being featured in the Gene Kelly film *Singing in the train*. Denis rejoined with a typed reference he once saw to the French singer Yes Montand, an opera billed as *Dr Rosenkavalier*, and a record list's *Herb Alpert and his Tijuana Bras*.

Within a few days of that conversation, Mr Joe Winstanley had written to me from Blackburn, having noticed a printed reference to Peter Dawson's recording of *O ruddier than the clergy*. (How Owen Brannigan would have loved that!) And it was the same Mr Winstanley who noticed a hoarding outside a theatre, on which two opera posters had been rather carelessly pasted up – or perhaps part of the sheet had been torn away. Anyway the lettering did not coincide as it should, with the result that the poster read:

MADAME BUTT DIE FLEDER FLY

A final word of thanks to our attractive and wonderfully efficient BBC secretary (and scorekeeper) Christine Hardman, who can type faultlessly when occasion demands, but who once gave me special delight with a line from the maudlin song *That old-fashioned mother of mine*, which according to Christine went:

'An old-fashioned bedside where she keels and prays . . .'

Etcetera

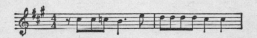

This chapter, being something of a dump for otherwise unclassified material, is headed *Etcetera*. Equally, it might have been described as a Miscellany. Even, as John threatens to call his autobiography, *Amiscellany*.

Not that only John is involved. The usual names all appear, together with those of one or two of our letter-writers. Mr and Mrs Bickles, for instance, of South Molton in Devonshire, who reported a delightful moment when their local amateur operatic society was rehearsing. Rushing in late for rehearsal, and rather flustered, a young member of the chorus said: 'I'm so sorry I've kept everybody waiting. But the man following me was walking so slowly!'

A matter for constant regret among our early listeners was the fact that for all David Franklin's reputation as a leading opera singer, none of his records remained in the catalogue by the time our series was under way. This was due partly to chance, and partly to the extraordinary practice the record companies have of removing records from sale almost at the moment of issue. (It is rumoured that one company inadvertently deleted a record from the catalogue three months before it was brought out.) David's historic Glyndebourne *Don Giovanni* lasted in print longer than most album recordings, but for all its historical importance I notice that it is now unavailable.

With that very recording in mind, I once asked David: *What was your best-paid professional engagement?*

The answer came instantly. 'It was the complete recording I made of *Don Giovanni* before the war. In those 78-r.p.m. days, singers were paid four pounds a side for gramophone work. I sang on four of the sides: total fee sixteen pounds.

'But when my cheque came I saw that it was for twenty pounds. Why? Then I realized. On side Five in the duet *O statue gentilissima*, the Don invites the statue to join him for supper. To his amazement the statue – that was me – answers him, and sings, 'Si'.

'One word – four pounds. For that split second I was the highest-paid singer on earth; not even Gigli got four pounds a note. But the trouble was that all the other notes were so cheap in comparison.'

Kurt Weill composed The Seven Deadly Sins. *What are they?*

According to Denis, they comprise lust (the one everybody thinks of first), envy, gluttony, greed, avarice, leaving your porch light on and parking on a double yellow line.

I told Denis that I had seen a rather touching sight a day or two before. At the Church of All Souls, Langham Place, a few yards from Broadcasting House, the vicar had decided to give a series of sermons, devoting each to one of the seven deadly sins. The sermons were listed, with dates, on a poster outside the church. One rather grey morning, on my way to the BBC, I had seen an elderly gentleman copying down the list of sins into a notebook. A sad thing, failing memory.

———

Lytton Strachey once offered a rather interesting speculation on where one should be when reading the works of certain authors. One should read Pope in a garden, he insisted; Herrick in an orchard; Shelley in a boat at sea. (Though in view of what happened to him, that is the last place I would want to read Shelley.)

Question: how about applying the Strachey Test to music? Where should one be, when listening to certain composers' works?

> John gave a typical *My Music* example of lightning thinking on one's feet. (All right then, not on one's feet, but while speaking.) 'I think,' he said, 'one should listen to Bach in church; *Tristan and Isolde* in bed; Beetles in lettuce . . .'
>
> Frank, verbally precise as ever, came up with 'Liszt on the Woolwich ferry'. Denis, carrying on the Shelley thought perhaps, merely added that the one tune it would be best *not* to hear on a ship is *Nearer my God to thee*.

———

When I read the title of an LP called *Everything you've always wanted to hear played on the Moog synthesizer*, I reflected that as far as some musicians' tastes are concerned it must be one of the shortest LPs in history. There isn't much they want to hear played on the Moog synthesizer except perhaps its final selection.

But never mind them. Which LP would the My Music *panellists find singularly uninviting?*

> IAN: 27 Variations on the *Eton boating song*, by Hans Werner Henze, played by the Zagreb Wind Ensemble.
> FRANK: An LP called *Norden sings Wagner*.
> To which I could only add something I actually ran into while staying at a hotel in Denver, Colorado, namely the massed instrumentalists of the World Piano-accordion Congress playing Ravel's *Bolero*. 'Follow that,' I said, and nobody could.

———

When we learnt our musical notation as children, we were told that the notes in the spaces of the bass clef were A C E and G, and that the best way to remember them was through a mnemonic: 'A Cow Eats Grass'. The whole thing seems a bit out of date when one thinks of today's children, who may not know what a cow is and seldom see any grass other than in a butcher's window. So an alternative is needed as a modern mnemonic for A C E G, or for that matter for the treble clef notes E G B D F. 'Every Good Boy Deserves Fish' (or Favour) – impossibly Victorian. Can you suggest something better?

For A C E G, instead of A Cow Eats Grass, Denis, having taken a few moments to reflect, offered three possibilities: 'Addinsell's Concerto Evokes Grieg's', 'Aberystwyth's Choirs Eschew Guitars', and – because we never seem to be able to keep sex out of it for long – 'Auntie Clara Entertains Gentlemen'.

Frank's E G B D F mnemonics began with a biblical list: 'Ecclesiastes Genesis Book of Numbers and De-Fesians', which is far-fetched even by Muir standards. Then he settled down and offered something infinitely more prosaic: 'Elasticated Ginger Beards Disconcert Ferrets'. I have an idea that is the mnemonic that would appeal most to today's children. Or perhaps on second thoughts, Frank's third thought: 'Erotic Gum Boots Delight Fetishists'.

In a later programme I asked Denis for a mnemonic that might be helpful for violinists who cannot remember the notes to which their four strings are tuned: G D A E. He suggested 'Gloomy Dane Aggravates Elsinore'. Having had much longer to think about it, I offered as an alternative: 'Gerald Durrell's Animals Ettim'.

———

Were you ever a disc jockey, Denis?

'Just once. I did a record programme for the BBC one Christmas morning and included a favourite of mine,

Frank Sinatra's *I've got a crush on you.* But I reckoned without the effect that record has on the housewives of Britain: it really must be the sexiest record ever made. I heard afterwards that quite a number of my lady listeners had been strangely affected as they cooked the Christmas dinner, in fact some of them stood in their kitchens crushing the turkey between their bare hands. One lady basted her elbow.'

How tall are you?

This may seem a curious question to ask in a musical quiz and in fact I never have asked it. I mention it because according to a BBC publicity hand-out, we are collectively the tallest panel in the history of panel games, totalling thirty-one feet in height. (All right then: 9.15 metres.) All of us are at or over six feet tall, with the exception of Ian, who is just under six foot on account of his having been fed on salted porridge as a baby. When we were discussing heights one evening, John Amis told us that when he first met Harry Secombe, that delightful Welshman looked up at him and said, 'I used to be like you once, but I was struck by a lift.'

Can you think of a musical riddle?

Denis managed to invent one on the spot. *Question:* What do you call a girl who thinks only of classical music? *Answer:* A symphomaniac.

In asking the question I had in mind the rather complicated, not to say long-winded, musical riddle that begins 'I gave my love a cherry . . .' But listeners duly contributed riddles of the standard question-and-answer kind;

one in particular which was popular in the old days of the music-hall and the Edwardian theatre. I had come across it before, but it was nice to be reminded of the once-topical:

> *Question:* Why was Haydn Coffin?
> *Answer:* Because he gave his Vesta Tilley.

– or if you prefer, because he gave his Vesta Victoria. I am inclined to think Vesta Tilley was the lady in the original, and this is confirmed by the sequel, sent in by one of our regular listener/viewers (and incidentally the first star I ever saw in person on the West-End stage), Binnie Hale. When Vesta Tilley married Sir Walter de Freece, wrote Binnie, the riddle grew another couplet and assumed four-line length:

Q: Why was Haydn Coffin?
A: Because he gave his Vesta Tilley.
Q: Why did he give his Vesta Tilley?
A: Because he didn't want the Lady de Freece.

———

Finally, can you think of an appropriate registration number for a musician's car?

Denis thought that Johann Strauss's car might have been registered 123 123, and Vincent Youmans's car would of course be T42. John suggested that a pianist specializing in Mozart concertos might enjoy having a car with the number K488. For a fiddle player Frank proposed V 10 L 1 N.

But Denis mystified us all with a car number for Wagner, which he insisted should be 9W. 'Why?' I asked obligingly. 'It was the answer that Wagner always used to give,' said Denis, 'whenever anyone said to him "Do you spell your name mit a V?"'

Appendix

Appendix 1

Key to the Musical Chapter-Headings

1. **OVERTURE AND BEGINNERS** (p. 9)

   These opening bars of the *My Music* signature tune were originated by the late Graham Dalley, and played by him on the mellotron. Some years later, when the original mono tape-recording almost literally wore out, a new stereo recording was made featuring brass and rhythm sections (with a good deal of new bossa nova material of my own) retaining merely the motto bars from Dalley's original. The similarity of these six notes to the first two bars of *Moon river* was surely inadvertent on Graham's part and is the kind of thing that happens to songwriters the world over.

2. **THE HISTORY OF MUSIC** (E. & O.E.) (p. 19)

   I like to think that when the medieval singer Iyan Warlis walked on stage to give his one-man mumming show, he would open with this well-known greeting, prior to favouring the audience with *Olde manne rivre*, *Ye road to Mandall Hay* and *Mudde*. The clef shown is my own invention and is intended to add a touch of period flavour.

3. **OPERA** (p. 33)

   No one expires more *fortissimo* than a prima donna, hence

my quotation, marked *fff*. It comes from almost any opera you care to think of, with the possible exception of *HMS Pinafore*.

4. POPERA (p. 53)

Here I have abandoned standard musical notation in favour of guitar symbols, as being more appropriate to the popular music world. The two chords illustrated are just about the easiest to find, and the beginner, having mastered them in the course of his first two or three months at the instrument, is then equipped to play most of the rock and roll favourites of the day.

People like myself who have reached the dawn of early middle-age will note a similarity between the design of a guitar symbol and the ukulele symbols which decorated the sheet music of our youth. ('Arranged by Alvin D. Keech.') I never had the pleasure of meeting Mr Keech, but he was just as much part of my growing years as Cherry Kearton, J. F. Horrabin (who created the Arkubs) and Mr Sturmey-Archer, manufacturer of the three-speed gears on my Raleigh bicycle.

5. OPS (p. 63)

The rather complex invention heading this chapter is an example of the dodecaphonic or twelve-tone movement in serious music, of which it has been truly said ... If John Amis were the chairman of *My Music*, and I were one of the panellists – which heaven forbid, because then I wouldn't have the answers written down in front of me – I think he might well close the programme on some such sequence of notes as this.

6. TRULY IT HAS BEEN SAID (p. 75)

This little musical motto has some Point, as G. and S. addicts laughingly tell one another, because it comes from *The Yeomen of the Guard* and is sung by the wandering Jester Jack. '*I've jibe and joke ...*'

7. THE CONDUCTOR IS ALWAYS RIGHT (p. 81)

That statement – 'the conductor is always right' – comes
from a story told by the gentle and entertaining per-
cussionist and lecturer, James Blades. Jimmy, as a young
lad beginning his first orchestral engagement, observed a
two-bar rest on his drum part and was promptly told by
the musical director to ignore it. 'When my arm comes
down you flog them drums, and you keep flogging 'em
until I stop,' said the musical director.

'I learnt at that moment the Golden Rule,' Jimmy
reported. 'The conductor is always right.'

Absolutely so. Even when his beat suggests that the
opening 5/4 bars of Tchaikovsky's 6th Symphony were
written in four time.

8. ONCE A PUN A TIME (p. 87)

No comment. Not even an apology.

9. WHAT ME? – SING? (p. 95)

I have taken the liberty of writing down what I think
Denis might sing if asked to render *Poor wandering one*.
Appropriate title too, now I come to think of it.

10. THE PIANO MEDLEYS (p. 105)

The bride is obviously Matilda.

11. COMPOSERS: THE TRUTH AT LAST (p. 109)

Any schoolgirl could tell you what this piece is called,
provided she had been a pupil at Josias Priest's School for
Young Gentlewomen in 1689–90. It comes from *Dido
and Aeneas* and is a setting of the line 'Destruction's our
delight . . .!' in Act 3 of Purcell's opera – though perhaps
'destruction' is a tough word to apply to our harmless
half-hour.

12. SO MUCH FOR JAZZ (p. 117)

This is the slightly jazzy bit from the second strain of the

My Music signature tune Mark 2, for which I claim the
blame. Musicians of my era (all right then, my type too)
call this rhythmic pattern for convenience 'a Charleston
beat', in honour of the 1920s dance commemorating the
town in West Virginia. Adding the word 'Charleston'
under each of these bars has ensured that in all royalty
statements I am credited as the lyric writer. I may only be
a naive country lad from East Anglia but I know my rights.

13. A FEW TECHNICALITIES (AND FOREIGN, TO BOOT)
(p. 123)

I'll bassoon explain this to anyone who hasn't recognized
it. The theme is Liszt's *Valse oubliée*, not to be confused
with the popular song *The little boy that Santa Claus
fagott*. The word *fagott* means . . . oh never mind.

14. MUSICAL MYSTERIES EXPLAINED (p. 131)

Elgar's enigmatic opening bars have defeated the Holme-
sian efforts of successive generations of musical detectives.
Speaking for myself (and I don't remember ever speaking
for anyone else) I am perfectly happy with the explanation
that Elgar's theme was founded on the 'Britons never
never never . . .' bars in *Rule Britannia*. It would be
characteristic of the man, and would explain why the
composer told Dora *Penny* that she 'of all people' should
be able to solve his enigma.

On the other hand by simply adding five words, as I
have done, one can put an entirely different complexion
on Elgar's reluctance to explain. (Especially in the
presence of C.A.E.)

15. SIR, YOU ERR (p. 143)

This bar and a half of operatic confusion takes longer to
explain than to sing. *Care selve* is an aria from Handel's
Atalanta. *Una voce poco fa* comes from Act 1 of Rossini's
The Barber of Seville. *Caro nome* (of which these are the
opening melody notes) is Gilda's aria in Act 1 Scene 2 of

Verdi's *Rigoletto*.

16. ETCETERA (p. 149)

The two bars quoted comes from Hugo Wolf's *Auch kleine Dinge*, which may be translated as 'little things can also delight us'. We boys at a school, rather less poetic in our phraseology, put it differently: 'Little things please little minds'. If the cap fits . . .

APPENDIX (p. 157)

As a tailpiece I have not unnaturally chosen the last movement theme of Haydn's Farewell Symphony. Was it from John Amis, or David Franklin, or perhaps Ian Wallace – or then again, was it from Frank Muir or from Denis Norden? – that I learnt that the doctor said to Haydn's mother when her baby was late arriving: 'What, a boy? Where are you, Haydn?'

Appendix 2

For *My Music* Collectors

In radio and television programmes dealing with antiques, Arthur Negus and his colleagues often say, of a given piece, 'they're very collectable'.

It seems that we of *My Music* are in some way 'very collectable'. Faithful followers all over the world, notably in Britain, Australia, New Zealand, South Africa, North America and Canada, regard us almost as their special property, and some, like Richard Marshall of Victoria in British Columbia and Dr Andrew Runswick of the University of Western Australia in Perth, claim scarcely to have missed a single edition.

For their benefit – and a little for ours, since it is interesting to see one's past life flash by without the necessity of drowning – I give below some facts and figures of the more than 300 editions of the programme which we had recorded, either for radio or for radio and simultaneous television, by the end of 1980.

VENUES

My Music's 'home' is the Commonwealth Institute Theatre in Kensington High Street, London, where we have recorded almost all our programmes since the early 1970s. The very first series was recorded nearby in the old Kensington Library Theatre before it was rebuilt, but we have also appeared in the

BBC's former Piccadilly studios, the Playhouse Theatre (now closed) at Charing Cross, Pebble Mill studios in Birmingham, and in the BBC's underground studio in Lower Regent Street, known as 'The Paris' because of its origins as a cinema showing French films. Other *My Music* visits have been to the Royal Academy of Music, the Senate House at London University, Birmingham Exhibition Centre, Cheltenham and Edinburgh Festivals and Sadler's Wells Theatre in London. Not all of these places have been acoustically ideal, but our engineers have triumphed over all odds: brilliant sound experts Ricky Merrett, Bob Harrison, Peter Brunskill, Pete Freshney and Stuart Taylor.

It is curious how the present recording of our shows simultaneously for radio and television seems to have puzzled many of our supporters. As each new BBC2 television series begins a new run, radio listeners write testily 'So! – You have deserted us for TV!' After a few weeks there is always a trickle of letters from viewers regretting that I should have found it necessary to have 'asked similar questions to the ones in the radio series last spring'.

I would have difficulty in doing anything else: the programmes are 'similar' because they are the same. Whatever Frank, Denis, Ian, John or I may say or do during the half-hour is at the same moment recorded for stereo radio and videotaped for television. Only the subsequent editing differs fractionally, being handled by Douglas Hespe and Tony Shryane according to the requirements of their respective media. Some ideas work well for radio; others work better for television.

The transmission plan remains broadly the same each year. The twenty-six programmes which we record two at a time on Thursday evenings from January to March are broadcast on Radio 4 during the first six months of the year, slightly later throughout the world on the BBC's External Services. At a later date in the same year, BBC2 television puts out its choice of thirteen programmes or so. In due course, BBC Transcriptions transfer the radio shows to disc, and offer each series for independent broadcast from far-flung radio stations around the world.

This wide span of transmission dates makes it essential that there should be no topical references in *My Music*. As far as we are concerned there is no such thing as a 'newly-opened show' or 'a recent TV serial'. The World Cup could never be mentioned, because by the time our programme is on the air in (say) Argentina, the cup might have changed hands and been won by Zaire (or even England). So it is that Beethoven centenaries tick by; heavyweight champions rise and fall; for us *The Sound of Music* is as fresh as next week's *Top of the Pops*. It is never winter or summer, day or night; the Prime Minister is The Prime Minister, whoever he or she may be. Hence cautious exchanges such as this:

> DENIS NORDEN (*trying to identify a piece of music*): Is it modern?
> ME (*cagily*): Relative to what?
> DENIS (*catching on*): Relative to Time, of course.

All four of my colleagues – Frank, Denis, John and Ian – know about these problems and as good professionals instinctively respect them, only rarely forgetting themselves and making some reference to 'last year' or 'this terrible weather' ... Though I have to admit that occasional references to bad weather have slipped through, without any complaints being received from our far-flung family of listeners. People on the whole are indulgent and forgiving. In a word, people are nice.

And that – like *My Music* itself – seems to be universal.

Appendix 3

Calendar

1966	31 July	First recording at 'Paris' Studio, Lower Regent Street, London.
1967	5 February	Lionel Hale stands in for Frank, who is indisposed.
1968	24 May	Michael Flanders for Frank.
1969	6 March	Barry Took for Frank.
1971	25 November	First *My Music* recording in stereo.
1972	25 May	Visit to Royal Academy of Music, in celebration of its 150th Anniversary. TV cameras present, to film inserts for a David Franklin programme *One Pair of Eyes*.
	5 July	First combined game *My Word, It's My Music!* jointly chaired by Sir Jack Longland and Steve Race, with combined panels including Dilys Powell and Anne Scott James.

	13 November	Recording at BBC Broadcasting Centre Pebble Mill, Birmingham, in celebration of BBC's 50th Anniversary.
1973	18 January	David Franklin's last appearance.
	25 January	Owen Brannigan OBE stands in for David Franklin.
	13 September	John Amis joins the panel.
	15 September	Second *My Word, It's My Music!*
1974	28 February	Alfred Marks stands in for the indisposed Frank Muir.
	7 March	Radio recording filmed by BBC-TV as an experiment. Producer: Douglas Hespe.
	27 April	Visit to Sadler's Wells Theatre, as part of the Lilian Baylis Century Festival.
1976	5 July	First visit to Cheltenham International Festival of Music.
1977	13 January	200th recorded radio programme. Also the first television recording to be subsequently transmitted (21 September).
	24 March	Royal visit, with HRH Prince Michael of Kent in the audience and subsequently backstage.
	7 April	Special edition in honour of the Queen's Silver Jubilee.
	21 May	Visit to London University.
1978	12 December	250th edition recorded (Commonwealth Institute).
1979	25 January	Barry Took stands in for Denis (indisposed).
	21 August	Edinburgh Festival.

1980	9 January	Bobby Jaye becomes executive producer.
	8 April	300th edition takes place during visit to Peebles Hydro for Conferance of the Incorporated Society of Musicians (President: Ian Wallace).
	14 June	Frank Muir and Dennis Norden each awarded the C.B.E. in the Queen's Birthday Honours List.
1981		*My Music* totters on confidently into the 1980s.

Index

MORE ABOUT PENGUINS
AND PELICANS

For further information about books available from Penguins please write to Dept EP, Penguin Books Ltd, Harmondsworth, Middlesex UB7 ODA.

In the U.S.A.: For a complete list of books available from Penguins in the United States write to Dept CS, Penguin Books, 625 Madison Avenue, New York, New York 10022.

In Canada: For a complete list of books available from Penguins in Canada write to Penguin Books Canada Ltd, 2801 John Street, Markham, Ontario L3R 1B4.

In Australia: For a complete list of books available from Penguins in Australia write to the Marketing Department, Penguin Books Australia Ltd, P.O. Box 257, Ringwood, Victoria 3134.